This book is dedicated to

Rosemond Curson Price

MASTERPIECES OF

ANCIENT

JEWELRY

Exquisite Objects from the Cradle of Civilization

by Judith Price
President of the National Jewelry Institute

RUNNING PRESS
PHILADELPHIA · LONDON

9   8   7   6   5   4   3   2   1

Digit on the right indicates the number of this printing

Library of Congress Control Number: 2008920409

ISBN 978-0-7624-3386-5

Cover and interior design by Corinda Cook
Edited by Kristen Green Wiewora
Special thanks to Melissa Wagner
Typography: Requiem, Univers, and Goudy

Running Press Book Publishers
2300 Chestnut Street
Philadelphia, PA 19103-4371

Visit us on the web!
www.runningpress.com

(Page 1)
Pair of Earrings
Byzantine, 6th century C.E.
Gold, pearls, emeralds
L: 4.3 cm
Private Collection

(Contents page)
Earring
Unknown, 16th to 15th century B.C.E.
Gold
The Israel Museum, Jerusalem
IMJ 2007. 17. 2

CONTENTS

ACKNOWLEDGMENTS

When I first began researching and writing *Masterpieces of Ancient Jewelry*, I could never have imagined the challenge and the journey. Even having graduated from the University of Pennsylvania and having done graduate work at Columbia did not adequately prepare me for the task; there was so much to learn. I had to start at the beginning, between the Tigris and Euphrates in the Garden of Eden, a place where three major religions began. More importantly, since this book is about jewelry, all references—whether political, economic, geographic, or cultural—needed to embrace that theme.

So many institutions and their experts have helped reconstruct such a complex mosaic of ancient civilizations. They include the Louvre in Paris and its President and Director-General, Henri Loyrette, and Dr. Béatrice André-Salvini, Director of the Ancient Near East Department; the Israel Museum in Jerusalem and its Director, James S. Snyder, its Curator of Chalcolithic and Canaanite Periods, Osnat Misch-Brandl, and its Senior Curator of Islamic Art and Archaeology, Na'ama Brosh; the Vorderasiatisches Museum, Staatliche Museen zu Berlin (the Museum of the Ancient Near East in Berlin) and its Director, Dr. Beate Salje, and its Deputy Director, Dr. Ralf B. Wartke; the Metropolitan Museum of Art in New York and its current Director and Chief Executive, Philippe de Montebello, and its Curator of the Department of Islamic Art, Dr. Stefano Carboni; and the Princeton University Art Museum and its Curator of Ancient Art, Dr. J. Michael Padgett.

Other important experts, lenders, and contributors to *Masterpieces* include Dr. Donny George Youkhanna, Professor of Anthropology at Stony Brook University; Dr. Karen Wilson, Kish Project Coordinator at the Field Museum; Dr. Renée Dreyfus, of the Fine Arts Museums of San Francisco; Dr. Barbara Deppert-Lippitz, expert in ancient jewelry; Dr. Aubrey Baadsgaard, of the University of Pennsylvania; James C. Sanders, of The Oriental Institute Computer Laboratory of the University of Chicago; the Louvre's Nicolas Bel; Christiane Fischer, President of AXA Art Insurance Corporation; Don Demaio; Bibiane Choi; David Behl; John Ortved; anonymous lenders; and Ali Aboutaam and Hicham Aboutaam, who encouraged me throughout this project with their knowledge.

When the exhibition opens at The Forbes Galleries, you will share the vision of our board member, Christopher Forbes, who three years ago believed the National Jewelry Institute belonged in the space previously occupied by the famous Fabergé eggs. You will also admire the work of designer Cleo Nichols whose creativity illuminated all our installations. Most importantly I would like to thank Ralph Esmerian, Curator of this extraordinary exhibition. The exhibition and the book was composed and produced under the supervision of NJI's Vice President, Lucia Suljic. Having worked with me for over ten years, and being a lawyer, she respects the details and deadlines required to stage such a major exhibition.

The National Jewelry Institute wishes to thank its sponsor, **Christian Dior Couture,** for its respect for tradition and vision for the future and its President, Chief Executive Officer, Sidney Toledano, for his spirit and support.

This exhibition would not have been possible without the generous support of the Vice Chairmen of the **International Council:** The Aboutaam Family; Jean-Christophe Bédos, President & CEO of Boucheron; John K. Castle; Phyllis and William Mack; Alan G. Quasha and Ilona Nemeth; Jonathan P. Rosen; and Dr. Axel Stawski.

Our Board is grateful to **AXA Art Insurance Corporation** for its continued sponsorship of all our exhibitions.

I finally must thank the very dedicated Board of Trustees of the National Jewelry Institute who have encouraged and guided the development of what will certainly be our most ambitious and successful exhibition: Ashton Hawkins, Chairman; Ralph Esmerian, Vice Chairman; Hervé Aaron; Yvonne Brunhammer; André Chervin; Christopher Forbes; Chantal Miller; and Peter O. Price.

INTRODUCTION

Men and women have adorned themselves with jewelry from the earliest times of nomadic life, when wild animals were first domesticated and land cultivated. These jeweled artifacts illuminate ancient culture and customs, enabling us to better understand the formation of society.

Some jeweled objects were worn as status symbols, while others were endowed with magic to ward off evil. In Ur, one of the earliest known civilizations, double spiral pendants found in a child's grave are believed by scholars to have been left by pregnant women to ward off evil. Lapis lazuli carved into frog-shaped amulets were also buried there to protect the mother's fertility. At the royal grave of Queen Pu-Abi in Ur, archeologists discovered an early example of a status symbol: her gold, lapis lazuli, and carnelian comb, which consisted of seven gold rosettes, whereas her handmaiden's comb, also found in Ur, had only four or five.

According to Jewish, Christian, and Muslim beliefs, the cradle of civilization was the Garden of Eden, recognized as the birthplace of their societies. The Jewish calendar marks the number of years since the Garden of Eden flourished. Although scholars of all faiths may debate the precise date and exact location of this paradise, most agree that the birth of all human civilization was located in Mesopotamia, at the cusp of that fertile crescent between the Tigris and Euphrates rivers, where the first cities and crafts developed long before the great civilizations of Egypt and Greece.

Masterpieces of Ancient Jewelry: Exquisite Objects from the Cradle of Civilization will provide a rich succession of masterpieces from the Ancient Near East, where civilization was born. These jeweled objects represent important historic collections from the world's great institutions: the Louvre in Paris, the Vorderasiatisches Museum in Berlin, the Israel Museum in Jerusalem, the Princeton University Art Museum in New Jersey, and the Metropolitan Museum of Art in New York. Because unauthorized excavations have been a thorny issue among historians, museums, and archaeologists, featured objects from private collections have been carefully vetted.

Masterpieces of Ancient Jewelry is organized chronologically, beginning with Mesopotamia, and followed by the Levant, Persia, Byzantium,

and Islam. To appreciate the role of jewelry, we must place it in the context of the culture during these periods. Maps, diagrams, and descriptions will delineate the relationships between and among emerging societies. Six thousand years ago, the inhabitants of the Near East were basically nomads whose national borders were loosely defined. Adding to the complexity are the shifting sands of hundreds of years of political and regional strife. But through the jewelry and the contributions of renowned archeologists, *Masterpieces of Ancient Jewelry* will transport the

reader to a time of the world's first kings, fortunes, cities, and wars.

Masterpieces also includes interviews with renowned archeologists: Dr. Donny George Youkhanna, who for many years was the Director of the National Museum of Iraq; Mrs. Osnat Misch-Brandl, Curator of Chalcolithic and Canaanite Periods at the Israel Museum in Jerusalem; Dr. Stefano Carboni, Curator of the Department of Islamic Art of the Metropolitan Museum of Art in New York; Dr. Barbara Deppert-Lippitz, an expert in ancient jewelry;

Dr. John Michael Padgett, Curator of Ancient Art at Princeton University Art Museum in New Jersey; Dr. Karen Wilson, Kish Project Manager at the Field Museum in Chicago; Dr. Renée Dreyfus, Curator of Ancient Art at the Fine Arts Museums of San Francisco; and Dr. Aubrey Baadsgaard, of the University of Pennsylvania's Department of Anthropology. These interviews will shed light on the enduring legacy of the Ancient Near East.

Let us begin by defining a "jeweled master-piece," which we generally describe today as a precious metal set with gems such as diamonds. However, because such precious elements were unavailable, the earliest ornaments from Meso-potamia were made from semiprecious stones

These disk-shaped rock crystal beads are styled in four single chains. The necklace clasps at the base of the neck and shows an almost regular scaling on the décolleté.

Necklace
Uruk, Layer III, late 4th to early 3rd
    millennium B.C.E
Rock crystal
L: 51 cm, 70 cm, 91 cm, 106 cm (appox.)
The State Museums of Berlin, Museum of the
    Ancient Near East
Inv.Nr.VA 11098

such as carnelian, rock crystal, and lapis lazuli; organic materials such as amber, bitumen, and shells; volcanic glass such as obsidian (black crystal); and gold. Today's gold jewelry is 14, 18, or 22 karats, but in ancient times, there were no alloys, so the gold used was as close as possible to pure gold, or 24 karat.

The featured masterpieces are a reflection of emerging civilization, when Mesopotamia produced the first literature, music, astronomy, and medicine. The invention of the wheel, the measurement of time, and even the first skyscraper (or ziggurat), were also products of Mesopotamia.

The story of *Masterpieces of Ancient Jewelry* begins with the discovery of the rock crystal necklaces at Uruk (or Tall al-Warka), a city on the Euphrates between 4000 and 3000 B.C.E. (Scholars have adopted B.C.E., "Before the Common Era" and C.E., "Common Era" in lieu of B.C. and A.D.). It was in Uruk that archaeologists unearthed the first evidence of writing. Thousands of clay tablets from around 3400 B.C.E. have been discovered, indicating that the Mesopotamians invented written communication. The

rock crystal bead necklace from Uruk, on the opposite page, while carved some six thousand years ago, is a masterpiece not because of its material, but because of the symmetry and craftsmanship of the necklace.

Uruk was the first and largest settlement in southern Mesopotamia. The invention of the wheel and the development of metal took place there. In the book of Genesis, Uruk is known as Ereck, home of King Gilgamesh who, according to legend, created the modern city of Uruk. In the mythical poem "The Epic of Gilgamesh" he begins his life as a narcissistic king who goes on a great adventure and finds, then loses, the key to immortality. Tablets portraying "The Epic of Gilgamesh" were excavated at Nineveh, picturing Gilgamesh wearing bracelets and amulets, demonstrating that both men and women wore jewelry. The story of Gilgamesh ends with his showing the ferryman his city of Uruk and its great city walls.

Also unearthed in Uruk were decorative cylindrical seals, crafted for use as identification tags or to tell a story. The seals are small (ap-

proximately two to six centimeters in length) and carved in reverse to leave a positive image when rolled on clay. Some seals were made in shell, metal, or stone, and they were often worn around the neck, much like today's "ID" necklaces. Later, Mesopotamian seals contained pictures of daily life or mythological subjects. Dr. Beate Salje, director of the Vorderasiastisches Museum in Berlin and an expert on the mythical cylindrical seals, relates that one of the earliest seals contained a recipe for making beer!

According to the book of Genesis, Ur, in southern Mesopotamia, is the birthplace of Abraham, and his birth (around 1800 B.C.E.) is cited by some scholars as the origin of Judaism. Eventually, Ur surpassed Uruk in development, establishing itself as a more prominent crucible of civilization. In the history of decorative arts and jewelry, Ur is best known from the excavations of archaeologist Sir Leonard Woolley. In 1922, on behalf of the British Museum and the University of Pennsylvania Museum, he unearthed the graves of the kings and queens who ruled during the mid-third millennium B.C.E. Woolley found more

than fifteen hundred pieces of extraordinary gold jewelry, the remains of wheeled vehicles, and musical instruments in gold, lapis lazuli, and wood. Gold objects in the tombs were created using techniques still practiced today, such as granulation, filigree, engraving, and fusion welding. Whatever the process, the results were impressive: combs for the hair, lapis lazuli dog collars, gold necklaces, and carnelian amulets for good luck. These objects may not rank as luxurious today, but they were quite precious in ancient times.

Ur and the other city-states in southern Mesopotamia shared the same language and gods, but these differed from the language and culture of the people of northern Mesopotamia, the Akkadians. By the middle of the second millennium B.C.E., the Akkadian king, Sargon, conquered the south and united the entire region. During this period, city-states rose and fell regularly. Rebellions and revolts were commonplace. Sargon's kingdom, Agade, in ancient Iraq, has never been discovered.

It was not until the era of Hammurabi, the sixth king of the Babylonian Dynasty, that, through war and conquest, the seat of power in Mesopotamia changed to Babylonia. It became the most important city in the Ancient Near East, home to Mesopotamia's largest skyscraper, and, most importantly, the origin of laws for the average citizen, known as the "Code of Hammurabi." The eight-foot monumental tablet on which the laws were written now resides in the Louvre. Today, people say, "an eye for an eye . . . a tooth for a tooth," without realizing they are quoting Hammurabi.

After Hammurabi died, there was a succession of revolts in the south. The warrior Assyrians made conquests across the Middle East, extending the domain of the Assyrian Empire, the first society to have an established army. Most of what we know of them comes from stone reliefs, not jewelry. However, jewelry that has been excavated from their graves shows a continuing fascination with carnelian and lapis lazuli. Often carnelian stones were strung with small seed pearls, or adorned with small silver earrings. From the excavations at Nimrud, also known as Kalakh, a stone Assyrian winged deity wearing a rosette bracelet as well as necklaces and a hanging earring surfaced. Though it is more common to see Assyrian deities wearing jewelry, these reliefs demonstrate that some soldiers did as well.

During the same period, beginning in the third millennium B.C.E., society was developing in the neighboring Levant, which consists of Israel, Lebanon, and Syria. Jewelry and the decorative arts of the Levant were an amalgam of influences from northern Mesopotamia. During this time,

semiprecious materials and metals were employed, such as carnelian, turquoise, and copper. Nearly one thousand years later trade developed between the Levant and Egypt, inspiring Egyptian styles and insignia in the Levant. Scarab rings became commonplace, and later scarabs were used as seals. Faience, an Egyptian process to make jewelry look like precious stones, was brought to the Levant. Subsequently, granulation, a jewelry technique where grains of gold are heated and attached to a gold background, was also adopted there. Examples of objects incorporating these techniques were discovered in the royal tombs at Ur as well as in excavations in the land of Canaan in the Levant.

It was the Phoenicians, the sea traders of the Levant, who exerted the greatest influence upon jewelry design. These great sailors from Canaan soon spread Mesopotamian culture all over the region. From the ninth century B.C.E., the Phoenicians, best known today for creating the modern alphabet, were also known as the "Purple People" since they extracted purple dye from snails located in Tyre (in Lebanon). They learned the secret of making pure glass and tinting it with purple, their favorite color. With the addition of oxides, hues resembling pearl colors were produced. Glass manufacturing was soon used to imitate colored stones, and colored mosaic glass vessels spread throughout the Mediterranean. Another Phoenician art form was the engraving of such gems as carnelian, rock crystal, lapis lazuli, sardonyx, and sapphires.

The Phoenicians established colonies in North Africa, Cyprus, Italy, and Spain. Many of these regions were rich in resources such as gold, silver, and copper. Phoenician and colonial craftsmen created gold jewelry and unique decorative objects using the popular techniques of granulation and filigree, often in themes pertaining to nature and religion. Animal motifs, rather than human forms, were more common.

Egyptian influence is evident in Phoenician jewelry design, from pendants modeled after the Egyptian Eye of Horus (to ward off evil and protect the wearer) to rings resembling designs of older Egyptian stone-carved finger rings. A golden Tree of Life pendant, pictured on the opposite page, incorporates natural and religious themes using birds and goats. It represents the tree of life in the Garden of Eden from

In the brief few years since its origin, the National Jewelry Institute has set a new benchmark in the creation of exhibitions that bring together priceless works of jewelry from sources ancient and modern, public and private. With their current project, the Institute is looking back to those cultures that are the very wellsprings of western civilization, to showcase nearly 150 objects that have retained their allure over an expanse of more than 5000 years.

This exhibition perfectly complements the work of the Field Museum, whose archaeologists and anthropologists have been deeply involved in Middle Eastern excavations since the early decades of the 20th century. The Museum's particular focus has been the ancient Mesopotamian city of Kish, thirty miles south of modern-day Baghdad on the northern alluvial plain of the Euphrates River. The city held an extraordinary position during the formative periods of Mesopotamian history, and was known to the people of the time as the first city to which "kingship descended from heaven" after the great flood that had destroyed the world.

While *Masterpieces of Ancient Jewelry* opens a window on the world of ancient Mesopotamian art and craft, the Field Museum helps to place that art in a cultural context and unfold the lives of the people who inhabited that world. We are pleased and proud to be a part of this major undertaking.

—John McCarter, President and CEO, Field Museum, Chicago

Genesis, and symbolizes immortality. Phoenician craftsmanship is evident in the fine detailing.

By mixing Egyptian and Assyrian styles, an important characteristic of their art, Phoenician artisans elevated jewelry to a new artistic level in the Levant. According to *The History of Art in Phoenicia and Its Dependencies*, written in 1885 by Georges Perrot and Charles Chipiez, geometrical and vegetable forms prevail in Phoenician work. Jewelry is created to enhance the man or woman wearing it and make him or her more beautiful. Jewelry should be worn in simple combinations of straight and curved lines.

Outside the Levant, Phoenician settlements had a major impact on many other cultures, especially in Greece. The Ancient Greeks incorporated Phoenician and Syrian designs into their art and jewelry. Immigrant goldsmiths from Phoenicia settled in Greece and revealed their secrets, adapting what was formerly an Egyptian style to make it more Greek. Likewise the Etruscans used Phoenician motifs in their jewelry, but they employed extensive use of granulation to make the jewelry more uniquely their own.

The style of this pendant suggests that it was made in a Phoenician colony in present-day Spain.

Pendant with Goats and Birds in Sacred Tree
Ibero-Phoenician, late 7th century to early 6th century B.C.E.
Gold
H: 8 cm, W: 4.8 cm
Museum Purchase, John Maclean Magie and Gertrude Magie Fund, 1956–1988
Princeton University Art Museum

The carnelian intaglio is set in a fabricated pie-dish bezel. It is engraved with a two-line Kufic inscription, *Ahmad Allah*, which means "Thanks to God".

Silver Finger Ring
Early Islam, 8th to 9th century C.E.
Silver, carnelian
H: 24 mm
Private Collection

Historians refer to this cross-cultural time as the "Orientalizing" period.

The eighth and ninth centuries B.C.E. are sometimes called the "Ivory Age of the Levant," when carving of ivory was one of the main industries of workshops in the prosperous cities of Syria, Phoenicia, and Palestine. After Assyria launched a successful campaign against the Phoenicians, Phoenician craftsmen were forced to produce refined ivories that decorated the palaces at Nimrud, the Assyrian capital.

In 550 B.C.E. the Ancient Near East, including the Levant, was united as the Persian Empire by Cyrus the Great. It became the largest empire the world had known, stretching all the way from Spain to China, an area physically as large as the United States. Persian rule consisted of three major dynasties: Achaemenid, Parthian, and Sassanian. The Persians accepted the diversity of their people and had little wish to impose their identity on others. They were also the first to create an international trading network, known as the Silk Road; they established artistic interchange between the nobles, priests, and landed gentry; and they introduced the concept of monotheism (Zoroastrianism), though they tolerated different religions. In particular, Cyrus II accepted the Jews and helped more than forty thousand people leave Babylonia and return to Jerusalem to rebuild their temple.

Animals are a popular theme in the jewelry and decorative arts of the Achaemenid Dynasty. Although most jewelry did not survive, an example of such an animal motif can be found in the lion's head plaques that were sewn onto a person's clothing, like the ones on page 69.

In 330 B.C.E Alexander the Great, one of the greatest military leaders in history, conquered Persia and proclaimed himself king, marking the end of the Achaemenid Dynasty. It was not until 247 B.C.E. that the next major Persian dynasty, the Parthians, expelled Alexander's successors. The Parthians were highly militaristic, excellent horsemen who began to actively trade with the East via their expansion of the Silk Route to China. The court and its rituals played an important role during this period. Ceremonial drinking horns, called rhytons, were introduced, and jewelry reflected the citizens' desire to display their new wealth. Jewelry during this time was an amalgam of Greek and Near Eastern design. Most jewelry was made of gold and used the iconography of Dionysus, the Greek god of wine, on everything from earrings to vessels. The Parthian regime lasted nearly five hundred years and was instrumental in expanding the Silk Road linking Persia with China.

In 224 C.E. Ardashir I crowned himself "King of Kings" of the Persians after conquering the Parthians and establishing the Sassanian Dynasty. During this time, Persia achieved the height of its economic and artistic power. Its kings were patrons of music, literature, philosophy, and all the arts. In the Sassanian period, jewelry and the decorative arts reached a new level. Sassanian jewelry glorified the royals and their court. Nationalism soared and Zoroastrianism became the official religion. The king adorned himself with necklaces and earrings, as did royal women and dancers of the court. Scenes of the royal courts, dances, banquets, and hunts appeared on decorative bowls, vessels, and plates.

During this same time period, in 306 C.E., Persia's nemesis, Constantine the Great, became the emperor of Rome and made Christianity the official religion of his realm. In 330 he made Constantinople (which, until then, had been called Byzantium) the official second capital of his Roman empire. This era, known as the early Byzantine period, was marked by fighting between the Persians and the early Christians.

This is sixth in a series of exhibitions organized by the National Jewelry Institute for which The FORBES Galleries have been privileged to provide a setting. It is also the most ambitious exhibition undertaken to date. Bringing together almost 150 pieces for a show is a daunting task under any circumstances, but when the works in question include priceless treasures thousands of years old coming from museums and private collections around the world, the effort involved is Herculean. Not only have these masterpieces from the cradle of civilization been brought together in a stunning exhibition but a dazzling, and perhaps more importantly, a very informative catalogue has been produced as well making these treasures available and understandable to a wider audience than ever before. The NJI's "Hercules" who made this all possible is its Founder and President, the indefatigable Judy Price. Her vision and enthusiasm have been the driving force behind the NJI, and The FORBES Galleries are happy to help further the NJI's mission.

—Christopher Forbes, Vice Chairman, FORBES Inc.

The crosscurrents of the two societies had a marked effect on jewelry and the decorative arts, making Byzantine jewelry distinctive. For example, since birds were a popular motif in the early dynasties of Persia, Byzantine nobles and the wealthy aristocracy kept peacocks on their estates to suggest a setting reminiscent of the Garden of Eden. Jewelry with the peacock motif was favored, as its growing a new tail each spring symbolizes renewal.

In the Byzantine period seed pearls were often attached to earrings or sewn onto clothing, continuing a tradition originating in 4000 B.C.E. Other materials, such as rock crystal, carnelian, amethyst, and lapis lazuli, continued to be used. Through the early Byzantine era, the law of the land, the Code of Justinian, contained laws that restricted the use of gold, pearls, and emeralds for those who were not members of the royal family or part of the royal court. Gold tableware, chamber pots, and burial offerings were prohibited to contain them; only gold coins, fillings, and women's rings were allowed. Size, artistic quality, and material of the jewelry always reflected the social rank of the owner. During this same period, when Christian motifs dominated jewelry and decorative objects, Jewish iconography was rare.

Masterpieces of Ancient Jewelry will conclude with the advent of Islam and its impact on jewelry and the decorative arts. In 622 C.E., the prophet Muhammad left his birth city of Mecca to found the first Islamic state in Medina. After his death in 632 C.E., Muhammad's followers soon conquered Iran, Mesopotamia, the Levant, Egypt, and North Africa, followed by Spain, Central Asia, and India. They continued to preach the concept of one god, or Allah, establishing not just a religion but a change in culture as well. Unlike previous periods, Islamic art did not evolve slowly; rather, art was created specifically for Muslims. The effect upon jewelry was significant.

The Qur'an, or Holy Book, in which Muhammad inscribed his illuminations reveals nothing about the aesthetic of jewelry, paintings, and sculpture. The origins of much Islamic jewelry can be traced to Greek and Roman designs that are combined with granulation and filigree work to make the objects uniquely Islamic.

Both Islamic men and women wore jewelry during the eleventh and twelfth centuries. Such public adornment of women was, in fact, common. While the chador robe is often associated with strict women's dress today, a simple veil was more prevalent in ancient times, as was the case with early Christian women. Islamic jewelry and decorative objects involved an emphasis on calligraphy, geometric designs, and animal representation. Simple forms like the circle, square, triangle, and four-sided polygon were the focus of design for many jewelry pieces. Such geometric patterns make Islamic jewelry, architecture, and carpets distinctive. Filigree was raised to its highest level but never added weight to the jewelry. Every attention was paid to details.

Few pieces of Islamic jewelry have been found that date prior to the eleventh century C.E.; according to Islamic tradition, objects were not buried with the dead, so little or no jewelry has survived. Most earlier objects were probably classified as Roman, Byzantine, or Sassanian.

However, the excavations at Nihavand in western Persia and Nishapur in Iran do provide examples. In this respect, the *Masterpieces* exhibition will bridge the millennia to illuminate how ancient arts and traditions have influenced modern times.

Masterpieces of Ancient Jewelry will be on display at The Forbes Galleries, 62 Fifth Avenue, New York, from September through December 2008. It will then travel to the Field Museum, 1400 Lake Shore Drive, Chicago, where it will reside from February through June 2009.

This is the National Jewelry Institute's third *Masterpieces* exhibition. The first exhibition, *Masterpieces of American Jewelry*, opened in New York and then traveled to London, Paris, and Pittsburgh. The second, *Masterpieces of French Jewelry*, traveled from New York to San Francisco. Our mission is to support the preservation and creation of fine jewelry. We are hopeful that those studying jewelry and the decorative arts will be able to expand their horizons with these books and exhibitions.

Origins of Jewelry from the Ancient World

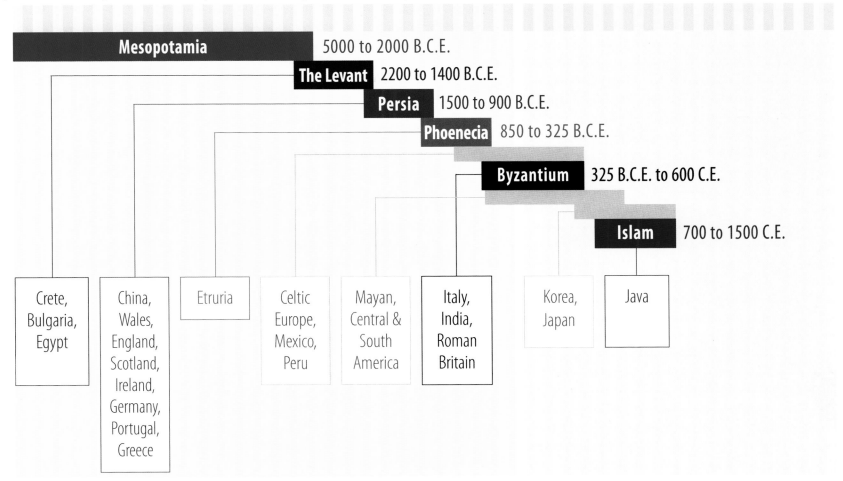

5,000	4,000	3,000	2,000	1,000	1,000	2,000

Mesopotamia 5000 to 2000 B.C.E.

The Levant 2200 to 1400 B.C.E.

Persia 1500 to 900 B.C.E.

Phoenecia 850 to 325 B.C.E.

Byzantium 325 B.C.E. to 600 C.E.

Islam 700 to 1500 C.E.

Crete, Bulgaria, Egypt

China, Wales, England, Scotland, Ireland, Germany, Portugal, Greece

Etruria

Celtic Europe, Mexico, Peru

Mayan, Central & South America

Italy, India, Roman Britain

Korea, Japan

Java

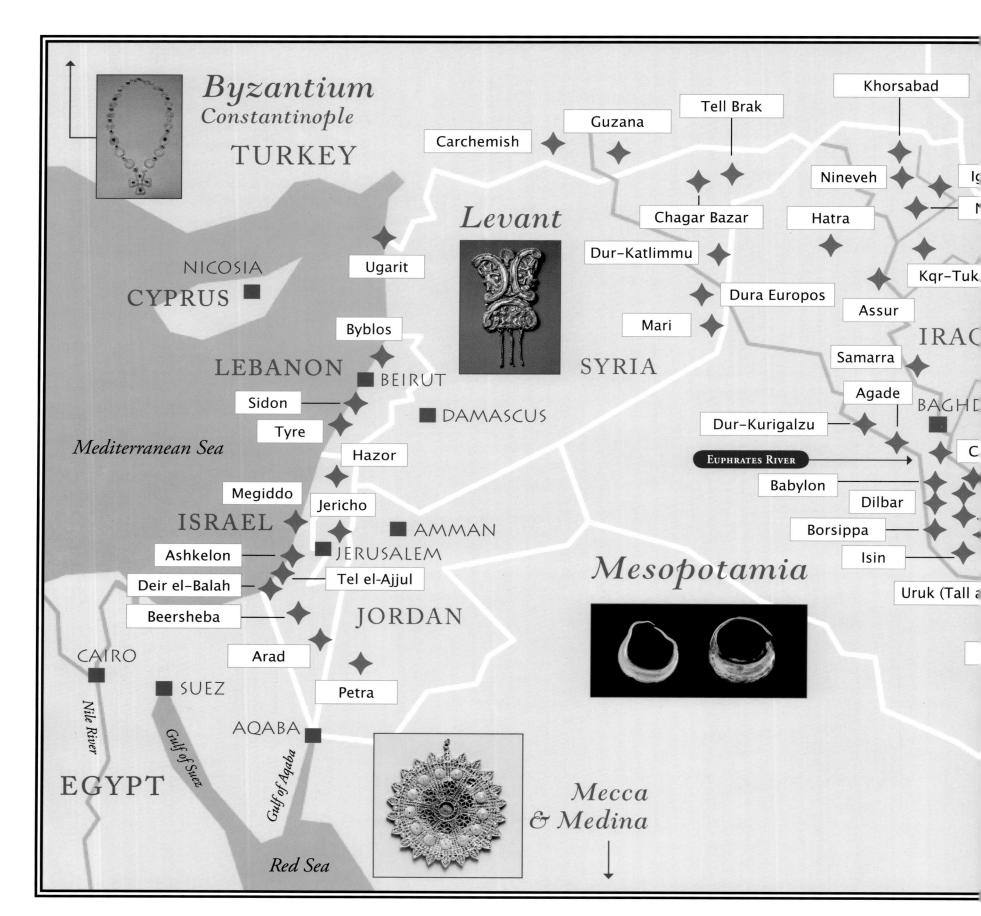

Byzantium
Constantinople

TURKEY

Khorsabad

Tell Brak

Guzana

Carchemish

Nineveh

Ig

N

Chagar Bazar

Hatra

Levant

Dur-Katlimmu

Kqr-Tuk

NICOSIA

CYPRUS

Assur

Ugarit

Dura Europos

IRAC

Mari

Byblos

SYRIA

Samarra

LEBANON

Agade

BAGHD

BEIRUT

Dur-Kurigalzu

Sidon

DAMASCUS

EUPHRATES RIVER

Tyre

Babylon

C

Mediterranean Sea

Hazor

Dilbar

Megiddo

Borsippa

Jericho

Mesopotamia

Isin

ISRAEL

AMMAN

Ashkelon

JERUSALEM

Uruk (Tall a

Deir el-Balah

Tel el-Ajjul

Beersheba

JORDAN

CAIRO

Arad

SUEZ

Petra

Nile River

AQABA

Gulf of Suez

Gulf of Aqaba

EGYPT

Mecca
& Medina

Red Sea

20

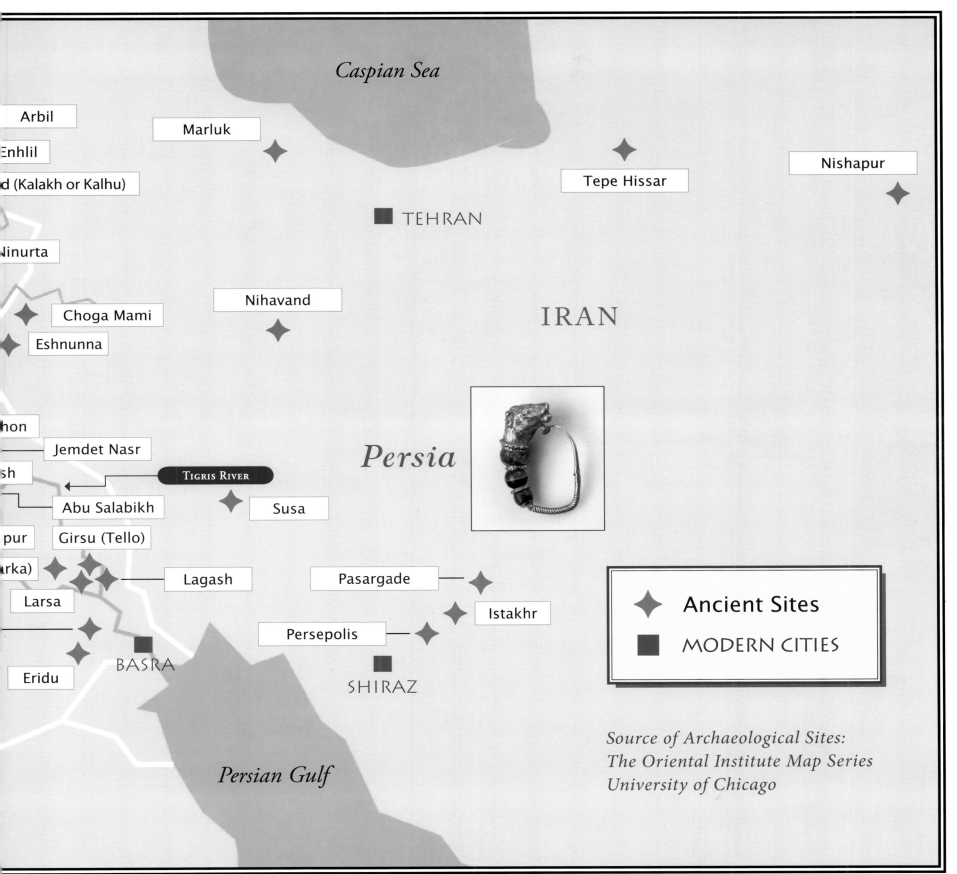

Caspian Sea

Arbil

Marluk

Enhlil

d (Kalakh or Kalhu)

Nishapur

Tepe Hissar

Ninurta

■ TEHRAN

Nihavand

IRAN

Choga Mami

Eshnunna

Persia

hon

Jemdet Nasr

sh

TIGRIS RIVER

Abu Salabikh

Susa

Girsu (Tello)

pur

rka)

Lagash

Pasargade

Larsa

Istakhr

Persepolis

■ BASRA

SHIRAZ

Eridu

Ancient Sites

■ MODERN CITIES

Source of Archaeological Sites:
The Oriental Institute Map Series
University of Chicago

Persian Gulf

MESOPOTAMIA

This extremely large pin (shown at actual size) was probably used to fasten a cloak. This shows the importance of animals in jewelry.

Pin with Two Wild Boars
Bactriane, 1900 B.C.E.
Silver
H: 12 cm
Musée du Louvre

Jewelry traces its origins to Mesopotamia, the Cradle of Civilization. Also known as the Fertile Crescent, the area is a huge arc in what is now known as the Middle East, stretching from the Tigris River in the east to the Mediterranean Sea in the west, and north from the Persian Gulf to the mountains of Armenia. It was there that humans first domesticated wild animals and cultivated land. At the beginning of the Neolithic Period, in the seventh millennium B.C.E., the world's first villages emerged in this area; during the following two thousand years, the villages grew into cities, and the first urban civilizations

formed. The structure and culture of that primitive society provides a context for the development of jewelry and the decorative arts.

The name "Mesopotamia" is derived from the Greek words *mesos* for "between" and *potomos* for "river," referring to the land between the Tigris and Euphrates Rivers. The inhabitants themselves never had a name for the entire region; rather, growing city-states were their reference points. Sumerian enclaves in the south, like Ur, Uruk, Lagash, Kish, Girsu, and Eridu, were important sites. To the north were the Semitic Akkadian cities such as Kalakh, also called Kalhu, (Nimrud in Arabic), Dur Shar-rukin (Khorsabad), and Nineveh (originally called Ninua).

In the third and fourth millennium B.C.E., Uruk was a major urban center, known for creating monumental stone architecture, early cylinder seals, and some of the first examples of writing. In 1912, German archaeologists began excavations of the ancient city. The most famous artifact, discovered in 1933, was the Warka Vase. It illustrates the structure of Mesopotamian society. The vase is dedicated to Uruk's most well-known patron, Inanna, the goddess of love and war. The alabaster base is carved with images spiraling upward, with a river at the bottom, animals on the next level, then citizens, priests, and finally gods at the top. In April 2003, the vase was looted from the National Museum of Iraq, and when it was returned to the Museum three months later, it was broken into fourteen pieces. Its current condition is not known.

During the same excavation in which the Warka Vase was found, archaeologists discovered objects made out of gold, silver, and copper,

These disc-shaped carnelian and rock crystal beads are arranged in an alternating modern presentation.

Necklace
Uruk, Layer III, late 4th to Early 3rd millennium B.C.E.
Rock crystal, carnelian
Approx. L: 100 cm (approx.)
The State Museums of Berlin, Museum of the Ancient Near East
Inv.Nr.VA 11078

as well as beads made from carnelian and rock crystal. The four single-chain rock crystal necklace featured on page 10 has been restored since the original find. The longest chain of the necklace is 3 feet 6 inches long, and the shortest is 20 inches. Its layered composition looks as modern today as it was nearly six thousand years ago. Shown above is another find from the German excavation of Uruk: a necklace approximately 36 inches long made up of alternating rock

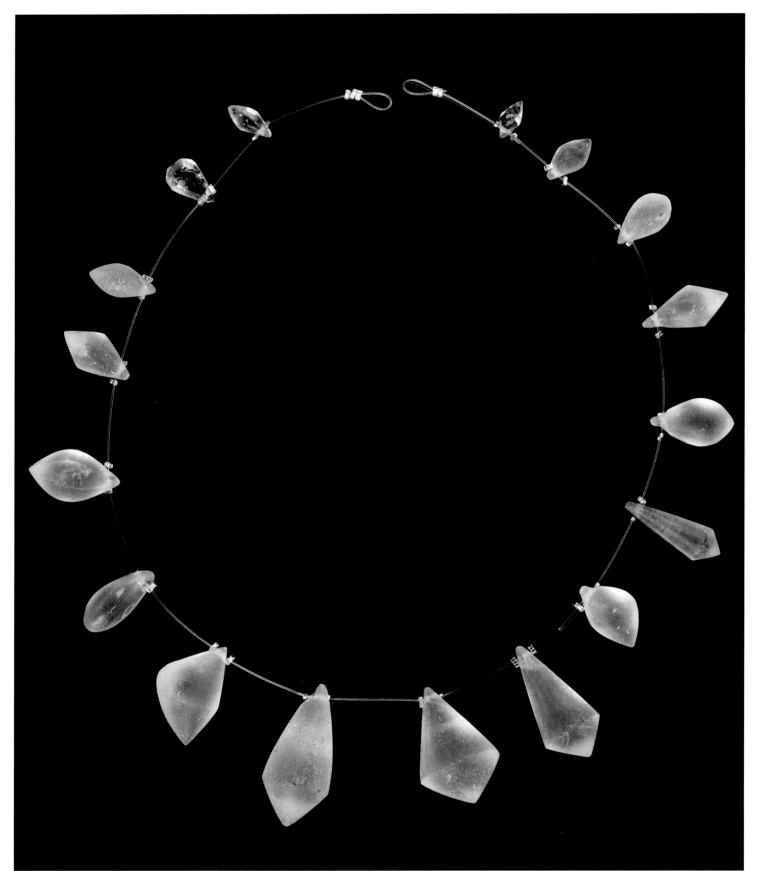

These almond-shaped beads made of rock crystal were invaluable ornaments worn by royalty at the top of the social hierarchy in Uruk.

Necklace
Tello, 3500 to 3100 B.C.E.
Rock crystal, quartz
L: 40 cm (approx.)
Musée du Louvre

variation in the sizes of the stones makes the jewelry timeless. In the original configuration, there would likely have been ceramic spacers. Who could imagine that this necklace was created as long ago as 3500 B.C.E.? The necklace is from Tello (formerly called Girsu), located near Uruk and Lagash, which are some of the earliest sites excavated by the French in 1877.

The necklace on this page, assembled with gold, carnelian, and lapis lazuli, is also from Tello, but it dates to 2600–2400 B.C.E. The accuracy of the composition of the necklace displayed today cannot be confirmed, but it is clear that the quality of the beads is extraordinary. The carnelian and lapis lazuli beads were created at great expense and generally reserved for royals.

In 1933, at an excavation site on the Euphrates River known as Tall Hariri, French archaeologists played a major role in discovering the ancient city of Mari. Here they brought to light the jewelry and cuneiform tablets from the Temple of Ishtar, the goddess of love and war. Although Mari was located in Syria, its position as a trading outpost for southern Mesopotamia

crystal and carnelian beads. Toward the bottom, the diameter of the rock crystal beads increases. Archaeologists believe that these two necklaces were votive offerings to the goddesses because of their length.

Rock crystal can have a very modern look, as evidenced in the almond-shaped rock crystal and quartz necklace on the opposite page. While the display of the crystal beads is contemporary, the

Though all early Mesopotamian beads are now strung on modern structures, the combination of the gold, carnelian, and lapis lazuli here is particularly interesting to the eye.

Necklace
Tello, 2600 to 2400 B.C.E.
Gold, carnelian, lapis lazuli
L: 35 cm (approx.)
Musée du Louvre

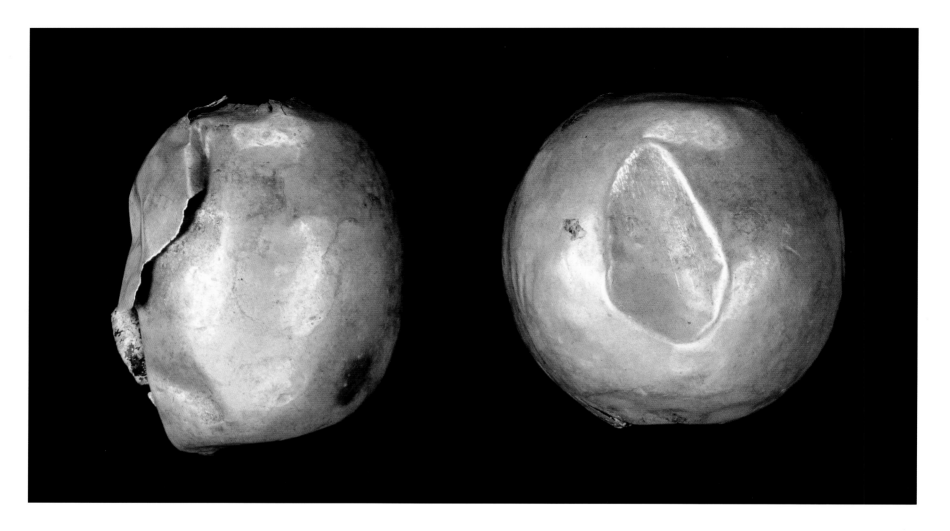

These beads are made of thin gold sheet plates over bitumen, a technique used to make large beads at a lower cost.

Pair of beads
Mari, Temple of Ishtar, early 2500 B.C.E.
Gold
L: 3 cm; D: 2.3 cm
Musée du Louvre

led it to be much more associated with Sumer. Mari's sculptures of gods and goddesses are recognizable by their big blue Egyptian-style eyes.

The two beads shown on this page, excavated from Mari, are made from gold sheets on top of bitumen, reinforced by a small bronze tube. With this technique, the creation of larger beads was relatively inexpensive. Beads created using this distinctive process were also found in the royal tombs at Ur. In fact, according to an

article authored by archaeologist Sir Max E. L. Mallowan, Agatha Christie's husband, there is evidence of close connections between Ur and Mari. The gold earrings shown on the opposite page, which were uncovered at the Palace of Mari, are also similar to gold crescent earrings discovered at Ur. Since the pin is thin, it may have been worn through the earlobe, or it is possible that it was placed around the entire ear. Mallowan believed that the jewelry found at Mari

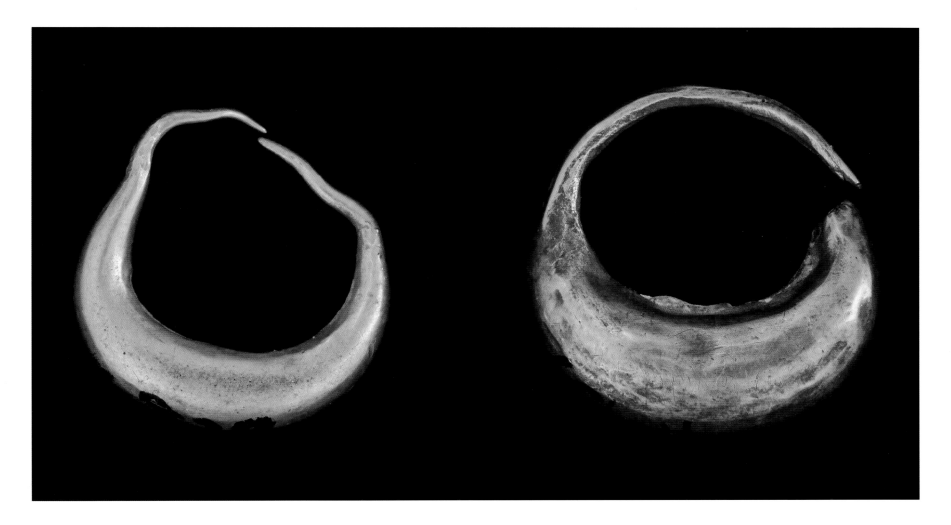

was part of a dowry belonging to a princess from Ur who was to be married to a Mari prince. Other pieces, like the necklace shown on page 28 were made with multicolored stones. It is interesting to note that some of the necklaces were worn by both men and women around the head or around the neck.

Beginning in about the third millennium B.C.E., amulets were worn to ward off evil or to promote fertility. Two such amulets, a bearded bull and a reclining calf, were excavated from Queen Pu-Abi's grave at Ur. Frogs and flies were important amulet motifs; page 29 shows a lapis lazuli frog, and a grey stone tortoise. The necklace on page 31, discovered in a ceramic jar in an infant's burial grave, consists of carnelian and agate. The center stone is in the shape of a frog amulet. The frog image was often used as a fertility symbol that was sometimes placed in the sarcophagus of a dead child to inspire a new birth. Another

These earrings were found in the Palace of Mari and are similar to earrings that were discovered at Ur.

Pair of Crescent-Shaped Earrings
Mari, 13th to 12th century B.C.E.
Gold
D: (left) 1.2 cm, (right) 1.3 cm
Musée du Louvre

Beaded Necklace
Mari, Tomb No. 133,
13th to 12th century B.C.E.
Various stones
L: 46 cm (approx.)
Musée du Louvre

The tombs of Mari contained several ornaments that were worn or used in the home. Necklaces like this one were worn either around the neck or the head.

Small amulets were either carried or integrated into collars and were used for protection. Amulets in the shape of fish, frogs or tortoises are associated with "Enki/Ea", the god of underground water, as well as wisdom. The eagle is related to the celestial world and the gods of war.

Frog-Shaped Amulet
Eshnunna, early 3rd
    millennium B.C.E.
Lapis lazuli
L: 1.3 cm, W: 1 cm
Musée du Louvre

Amulet in the Shape
    of an Eagle with
    Outstretched Wings
Tello, early 3rd millen-
    nium B.C.E.
Shell
L: 1.8 cm, W: 1.5 cm
Musée du Louvre

Tortoise-Shaped Amulet
Tello, early 3rd millennium B.C.E.
Gray stone
L: 2.5 cm, W: 1.6 cm
Musée du Louvre

The eyes of this lapis lazuli pendant in the shape of a ram's head are inlaid with gold circles. The bottom of the jaw, horns, and nostrils have incised details.

Pendant in the Shape of a Ram's Head
Sumer, 2900 to 2500 B.C.E.
Lapis lazuli, gold
H: 3 cm
Bequest of Norbert Schimmel, New York,
to American Friends of the Israel Museum
The Israel Museum, Jerusalem
IMJ 91.71.286

animal motif in Mesopotamian history is that of the eagle, an example of which can be found on page 29. As late as 850 B.C.E., eagle-headed demons were depicted in Assyrian reliefs. Amulets are an integral part of the multi-strand necklace on page 32. Reminiscent of a necklace created in America's southwest, the amulets represent everyday objects.

The photograph on page 33 is of a string of beads made from fired and glazed steatite. Steatite, also known as soapstone, is high in talc and rich in magnesium. It feels soft to the touch,

Necklace
Uruk, 1st millennium B.C.E.
Carnelian, agate, Egyptian Blue
L: 28 cm (approx.)
The State Museums of Berlin,
   Museum of the Ancient Near East
Inv.Nr. VA16727

This necklace was found in a ceramic jar in Uruk, as part of the burial gifts for an infant.
A frog-shaped amulet was often used as a symbol of new beginnings for the mother.

This necklace consists of ten rows
of beads with amulets representing
objects in everyday life.

Necklace
Susa, 3600 to 3100 B.C.E.
Limestone, shale
L: 62 cm; W: 21.5 cm
Musée du Louvre

and Native Americans as well as Mesopotamians made sculptures from it. During the third millennium, Tepe Yahya in Iran was a center for steatite production. For use in jewelry, the material was cut into various widths, glazed, and then heated to make it extremely hard, helping the glaze to adhere to it. Soapstone was also used to create the double-sided pendant on page 36. One side of the pendant shows a person with raised arms who is under attack. Both sides of the pendant features an animal with a dragon's head.

This string of beads made from steatite, often called soapstone, is typical of this period.

Necklace
Afghanistan, late 3rd millenium to
early 2nd millennium
Steatite, ceramic
L: 70 cm
Musée du Louvre

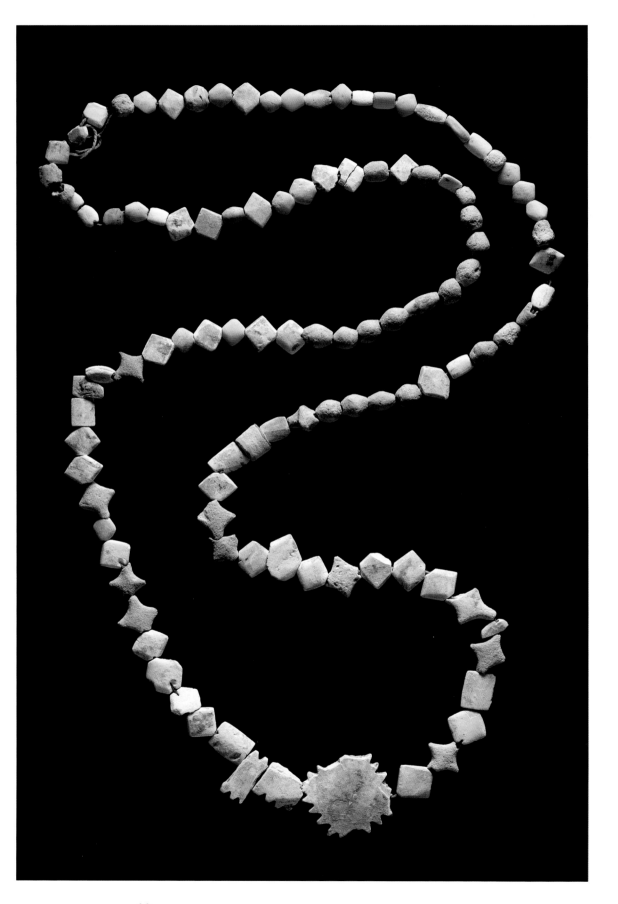

DR. DONNY GEORGE YOUKHANNA

Donny George Youkhanna

is internationally known for recovering thousands of priceless relics in Iraq. He is the former Director General of the National Museum in Baghdad and former Chairman of the State Board of Antiquities and Heritage. He is currently a visiting professor at Stony Brook University. Dr. George has a B.A. in archaeology and an M.S. and Ph.D. in prehistoric archaeology from the University of Baghdad. He is the author of two books on the architecture and stone industries of Tell Es-Sawaan, and he lectures around the world on the current archaeological and museum conditions in Iraq.

Do you believe there was a Garden of Eden, and if so, where was it?

After thirty years of working in antiquities in Mesopotamia, I really believe the whole of Mesopotamia was the Garden of Eden, because of what the people had achieved there. And speaking specifically of the works of art that we have, from the Sumerian times until the Islamic times, I am speaking about very high standards of literature and writing and the responsibility of documenting everything on cuneiform tablets. If you go into the south of Iraq, there is a very, very beautiful place where the Tigris and Euphrates meet and then flow down to Shatt al-Arab and go to the Gulf. It's a beautiful place, but there is another place called Fhood. I've been there. We were just passing by. It's a place in the heart of the marshes, and I stopped the driver and I said, "Let me go down here and see what's over here." When I came down from the car, I said, "My God, this is Eden," because you could see fields and fields of date palms and then the water. You could see the fish in the water; you could hear the birds singing all over there. I mean, what kind of heaven can be if it's not like that? So, I really believe that whatever was written, maybe the people have seen it and felt it and lived it—this is why they call that place the Garden of Eden.

What do you believe was the first civilization in the Ancient Near East? How did the people dress and adorn themselves?

We always believed that Mesopotamian and Egyptian civilizations in the Middle East were the first ones, but we do have specific evidence to suggest that Mesopotamian people were before the Egyptian. What the Mesopotamian people dressed and wore—they used everything—all kinds of fabric. I found evidence for textiles from about 5500 B.C.E., taking the history of textile 500 years back—older than we knew. So, they did have this kind of textile. They used material for their garments. We know, for sure, from the Royal Cemetery of Ur, there were beautiful garments. They had gold and silver material, and musical instruments decorated with shell and gold. They had great taste. More beauty to note were the treasures found in the city of Nimrud in 1989, where we found four graves of four or five queens and princesses from the Assyrian period. One of them was almost empty, but all three of the others were full of material and jewelry—material that no one would ever believe was made 2,800 years before the present time. The technology and the styles were splendid. That period was the peak of the

34

Assyrian Empire. They had excellent craftsmen who lived and worked in palace quarters.

When one looks at, say, an exhibition of King Tutankhamun's tomb, why is it more elaborate to the untrained eye than burial artifacts of Mesopotamia?

The philosophy of the Sumerians and Babylonians and Assyrians about gifts or grave goods was completely different. The Egyptians would put valuables in the graves so that the king or queen could use them in his other life. But we know that Mesopotamian people believed in only one life. The expression was *ana kur nu gi* ("they would go to the land and never come back"). That explains why they had very little buried with them in their graves. The Egyptians took all these jewelries and presents with them for the gods of the nether land to have mercy on their souls. They believed that their souls, not their bodies, were their essence as human beings.

What do you think is the greatest mystery remaining in terms of an undiscovered archaeological wonder?

There are two. One of them is the famous capital of the Akkadians, Akkad. We know a lot about it, but we don't know where it is. I believe that if we find it we will make huge strides in the history of the Akkadians, and we will uncover any number of works of art. We know that the Akkadians lived there around 2340 B.C.E.

The second thing, if we could discover it, is the grave of King Gilgamesh. We know it's full of

wonders and works of art. We know that when he died the people of Uruk cut off the Tigris River and built his grave at the bottom of the river. They diverted the river until they could build this grave. They buried Gilgamesh there, and then they re-opened the river. They thought that Gilgamesh was like the river, flowing all the time, and giving them hope for life to continue. The river has not changed its course for more than 5,000 years. So, that will be something to discover. The Belgians and the Germans have been doing some good work looking for the grave of Gilgamesh, but nobody has found it.

To preserve the art from Iraq or from Mesopotamia, should it be kept in the Middle East, or should it be kept in the Western world?

This is a tough question, but I do believe that it is not only an issue of Iraq or the Middle East. I believe that these works of art should be kept in their original countries. If you go to the Metropolitan Museum of Art and see the Winged Bull from Nineveh, or from Khorsabad, all you see is just one piece of art in the middle of New York. But, if people from New York go to Mesopotamia, go to Nineveh, or go to Nimrud, or go to Khorsabad, they would see this piece in its situation—they would see it, this wonder of art, as it was actually put there by the original people who produced that piece. We know that the Assyrians cut winged bulls in the quarries. They brought them to the cities by rafts on the river. On rolls they would bring them to the palaces and cities and put them in the entrances, then do the final

finishing there. They should not be removed again. If you go there you can understand the beauty of each piece. I believe museums all over the world should loan from one to another. It is a good interaction between two civilizations, between two museums, between two peoples, thereby averting the looting.

What's happening with the museum in Iraq?

It's completely closed. All the doors that can lead to the storerooms are welded shut. It happened in June 2006. We heard about an Iraqi security force operation in the street. Then camouflaged cars and people in uniform wearing ski masks came and kidnapped fifty people from the street of the Museum itself. We heard that the Ministry of Interior, responsible for the security of the city, was called, and they said, "We don't know these people and we don't know anything about this operation." For me it was a big surprise. I called for my senior staff. I asked them, "What can we do if these people come into the Museum, forcing themselves into these storerooms? Whatever they can take, can we stop them?" Everybody replied, "No." I said, "Okay, let's take everything we have in the offices and the laboratories and the registrations down to the cellars of the Museum and start closing them." In one day and a half we did that. Even now the museum is completely sealed; even the area of the administration is not open. It is a hard situation, but it's better than having materials stolen or looted.

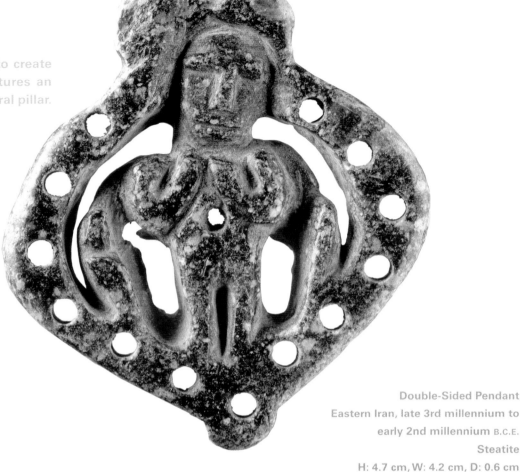

The ancient cities of Mesopotamia established the first rules for organizing life, religion, and social status. It was in Mesopotamia that literature, music, astronomy, education, medicine, and architecture were born. Even the invention of the wheel and the measurement of time are attributed to this place and period in history.

The central architectural element of the Mesopotamian cities was the ziggurat, a terraced brick pyramid of successively smaller rectangular stories. Architects note that Frank Lloyd Wright's Guggenheim Museum was built to look like an inverted ziggurat. Ramps descended from a shrine at the top of the ziggurat to facilitate the gods' arrival on Earth during festivals. The receding lower levels were often painted different colors. Unlike similiar works in Egypt, these ziggurats were never used as tombs for the Mesopotamians;

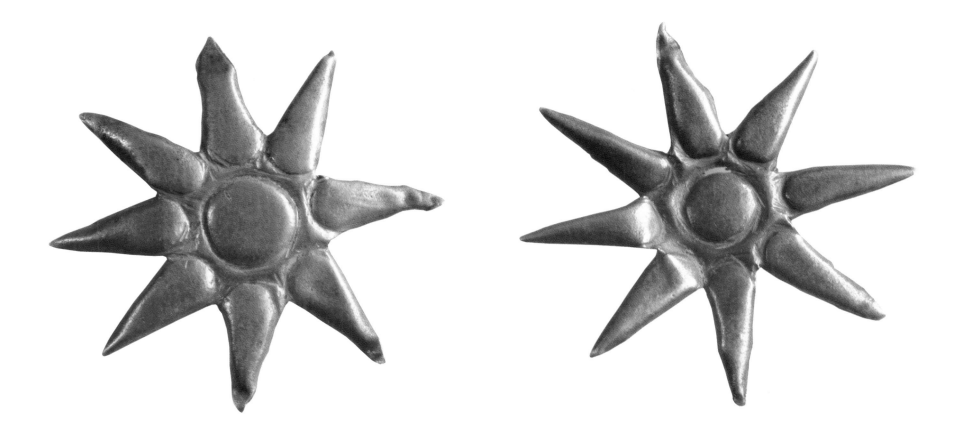

also unlike the Egyptians, Mesopotamians did not consider their king a deity, but rather only a representative of the gods.

In 2300 B.C.E. the northern ruler, Sargon the Great, conquered Sumer and renamed it Babylonia. Sargon then made Agade the capital. In today's terms, his Mesopotamian kingdom extended from Turkey through the Persian Gulf in the south, and through Iran to Syria in the west.

Mesopotamian society was divided into classes. There were the kings who represented the gods on earth, the priests who served the gods, the patricians who owned land, the working population of merchants and farmers who did not own land, and the lowest-ranked— the slaves. Marriage and family united each class of the community.

Prenuptial laws originated in Mesopotamia. Under the Code of Hammurabi, the first king of the Babylonian Empire, a marriage contract was essential. It was accompanied by strict rules of behavior. For example, if the wife could not bear a child, the husband could divorce her, but he

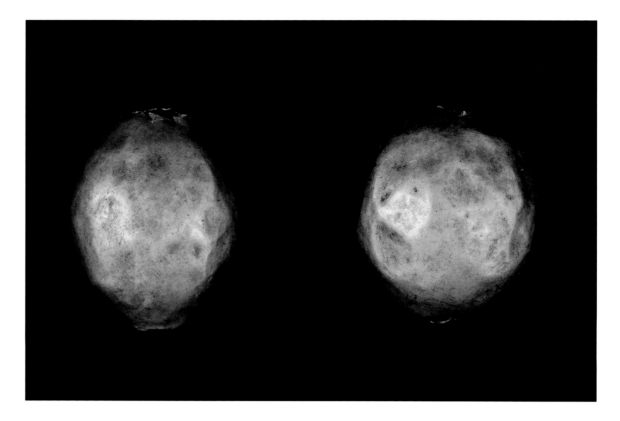

Beads
Mari, 13th-12th century B.C.E.
Gold, bitumen
L: 1.2 cm, D: 1 cm
Musée du Louvre

would need to "pay a settlement equal to the value of the gifts he gave her father when they married, plus the dowry she brought from her father's house."

Because the king was responsible for order on the behalf of the gods, the Code of Hammurabi was accepted. It was inscribed on a seven-and-a-half-foot-high stone column for all the citizens to read. Education and schooling were part of Mesopotamian culture, so most citizens were literate and understood the harsh penalties inscribed in the column. Examples from Hammurabi's Code include an "eye for an eye . . . ;" "if a free person kidnaps the son of another free person, the kidnapper shall be executed;" and "if a free person accuses another free person of murder but cannot prove the charge in court, the one who makes the accusation shall be executed." Today the column rests in the Louvre in Paris.

Hammurabi's Code provides insight as to how gods and kings dressed. On the stone we see Hammurabi dressed in a long gown draped over one shoulder while the god (Marduk) is wearing a five-layer shirt. The king and the god are both wearing jewelry, typical in Mesopotamia.

Necklace
Uruk, circa 500 B.C.E.
Rock crystal, carnelian,
    agate, lapis lazuli
L: 32 cm (approx.)
The State Museums of Berlin,
    Museum of the Ancient Near East
Inv. Nr. VA16729

This small necklace consists of colored beads and is typical of the type generally given to the deceased.

Karen L. Wilson is the former Director of the Oriental Institute Museum in Chicago and former Curator of the Edgar and Deborah Jannotta Mesopotamian Gallery. Dr. Wilson holds an A.B. in fine arts from Radcliffe College, Harvard University, and an M.A. and Ph.D. from the Institute of Fine Arts at New York University. While there, Dr. Wilson was the director of the excavations at Mendes, Egypt, and at Tell Genj, Iraq, for the Institute of Fine Arts. Dr. Wilson joined the staff of Chicago's Field Museum as Kish Project Coordinator and is currently a research associate at the Oriental Institute in Chicago.

What was the unique significance of Kish in the landscape of the Ancient Near East?

Kish was considered the oldest city after the floods that destroyed the world. Kish was also home to the first kings of Mesopotamia, whose kingship was said to descend from Heaven.

Why did the Field Museum initially make the decision to excavate at Kish from 1923 to 1933?

We do not know why exactly they chose Kish—perhaps because it is very large and consists of about forty mounds, or because it is not far from Babylon, with all of its biblical significance. Immediately uncovered at the site were bricks and stone vessels with royal inscriptions on them.

Did people in Kish wear jewelry?

They did wear jewelry. Both men and women wore jewelry, and both wore makeup, including eyeliner. People were buried with containers of the same black kohl used by Egyptians. Like modern Middle Eastern women today, they used it as eyeliner.

What were some of the customs in Kish?

Burials tell us a lot about customs in the ancient world. People were laid in the ground with their jewelry and cosmetics, as well as vessels of food and drink for them in the underworld. It was similar to the Egyptian customs, but we haven't yet found intact royal tombs.

Why were cylinder seals significant?

They are the most beautiful things on the face of the earth. They are little stone cylinders—maybe an inch and a half tall and half an inch in diameter, with scenes engraved on them. Ancients used them to roll over clay legal documents or sealings. There are scenes of wild animals, warfare, and mythology.

Tell us about the lion from Mesopotamia that recently sold at Sotheby's for $57 million.

It is one of the most beautiful things that has come out of the Near East. It is very hard to find things of that quality, with a pedigree, that have been out of the Middle East for decades. A pedigree is important if you want to be sure that no one is going to claim ownership and want it back.

Tell us about the life and the dress in the cities.

Mesopotamia was a country of many city-states. So, it was essentially an urban culture. Differences in dress would have reflected things like social status, occupation, or whether you were a member of the priesthood. It might also reflect which part of the country you came from. For example, we know that women from the north in Assyria wore their hair up in a kind of turban. Mesopotamian women seem to have put great big pins in their hair, like Japanese geishas do.

Tell us about the gods, the priests, and the temples.

There were a multitude of gods and goddesses, most of whom started out as embodiments of forces in nature, like storms, animals, or celestial bodies. Each god and goddess had his or her own temple, which was considered a home. The Mesopotamians actually believed that the god or the goddess was present in the cult statue, so the cult statue was treated as an upper-class resident in a temple.

How big were these temples?

They ranged from being one room to huge complexes of four or five different buildings with a ziggurat. The ziggurat was a temple tower. There seems to have been only one ziggurat in each city, even though there were many temples for many gods and goddesses. Each city had its main deity, and that would be the one in whose temple the ziggurat would stand. It was the goddess Inanna in Warka, and it was the moon god Nanna at Ur. Kish had a ziggurat, probably to the goddess Inanna. Inanna was, at times, the goddess of love, or the goddess of war, as well as the goddess of fertility.

Once the main deity was established, could it be changed?

Mesopotamian temples seem to have sat on the same spots for thousands of years, dedicated to the same deity. There is a very, very strong tradition of continuity. People would bring offerings to the temple for the priest to present them to the god or goddess. On cylinder seals are representations of a worshiper being led into the presence of a god or goddess, presumably into the presence of the statue. We also have representations of people carrying animals like sheep and goats, presumably as offerings.

What is the focus of your work regarding Kish today?

We are trying to publish the results of the excavation that took place from 1923 to 1933. This should take about two years. We have various scholars working on different aspects of it. It is not possible to go back to Kish right now; the area is just too torn up by conflict.

What is your favorite piece from Kish out of the 13,000 objects and 4,000 flint tools?

The piece that everyone loves most is a copper stand, coming from one of the tombs, which probably supported a beaker. It is in the form of a frog with a tall pole on his back. He was on display at the Metropolitan Museum of Art for decades. We brought him back because of this project. He is so appealing. On the bottom of this stand is a little frog with these white stone eyes. The whites have never really been analyzed, but they are probably made of gypsum, as was most Mesopotamian stone that was not imported. On the pole there are three prongs that probably held something. I think what went on top was a stone goblet. This cup holder, from about 2700 B.C.E., was found in the tomb of someone who could afford such a valuable object.

Stand Supported by the Figure of a Frog
Kish East, Ingharra, Early Dynastic Period
Copper alloy, stone
L: 13.4 cm; W: 14.8 cm; H: 48 cm
Field Museum, Chicago

The beads in this necklace were found
in a grave in Assur. Some of the beads
exhibit irregular forms and planes.

Necklace
Assur, 14th to 13th century B.C.E.
Carnelian, agate, black and white limestone
L: 39 cm (approx.)
The State Museums of Berlin, Museum of the Ancient Near East
Inv.Nr. VA Ass. 4832

Assur, also known as Ashur, was one of the capitals of ancient Assyria in northern Mesopotamia. The kingdom of Assur came to an end when Hammurabi incorporated it into his kingdom. During an exploration begun in 1898 by German archaeologists, a grave was found that contained gold finger rings and earrings. The beaded necklace on page 42 consists of carnelian, agate, and black and white limestone, and was also discovered in that excavation. The lower end of the necklace has a beautifully polished and banded agate stone. Also found in the grave excavation was the carnelian, agate, and lapis lazuli necklace on this page. The necklace is dominated by the alternating agate and carnelian beads and is enhanced by the polished surface of the carnelian, which is so translucent that its drilled holes are visible. The three-ply pendant is not only beautifully cut, but the design of the bright red carnelian bead is unusual.

Necklace
Assur, 14th to 13th century B.C.E.
Carnelian, agate, lapis lazuli
L: 98 cm (approx.)
The State Museums of Berlin,
  Museum of the Ancient Near East
Inv.Nr. VA Ass. 4241

This necklace was found in a southeastern sepulcher, a burial chamber used in ancient practices. There are places in this necklace where the beads are so transparent that the cut and polished surfaces of the drilled holes are visible.

In the Neo-Assyrian period, the Assyrian capital moved from Assur to Kalakh (Nimrud). German archaeologists discovered Assyrian objects that originated in the ninth through the seventh centuries B.C.E., including colored stones that were recovered from a burial site and restrung into three single necklaces. One of these, shown here, attracts attention because of the interplay between the blue lapis lazuli and the red carnelian beads. Archeologists also uncovered silver earrings, like the ones on the opposite page. These are characterized by a lunar crescent ring with a single cone pendant soldered onto it. Triple-cone earrings were also discovered.

This unique necklace shows off the color pattern of the carnelian and lapis lazuli beads.

Necklace
Assur, 9th to 7th century B.C.E.
Carnelian, agate, lapis lazuli
L: 61 cm (approx.)
The State Museums of Berlin,
    Museum of the Ancient Near East
Inv.Nr. VA. Ass. 4242.1

It is clear from evidence documented by the work of great archaeologists and scholars that Mesopotamia was the wellspring of civilization in the West, if not the world. Foraging became farming; nomads became citizens whose rituals evolved into organized religions. Villages grew into cities with structured societies whose customs and craftsmen developed jewelry from glass and carnelian, then imported metals, and eventually precious stones. Let us now turn to those successive periods and peoples who were so influenced by Mesopotamia—and who in turn exerted their cultures upon the world.

This assortment of earrings was part of the burial gifts found in a pottery sarcophagus in Assur, the original capital of ancient Assyria. The earrings have a crescent shape with a soldered cone pendant.

Six Earrings
Assur, 9th to 7th centuries B.C.E.
Silver
H: 2.2 cm, W: 1.8 cm (approx.)
The State Museums of Berlin,
    Museum of the Ancient Near East
Inv. Nr. VA Ass. 4242.4-9

THE LEVANT

The term *Levant* is derived from middle French, and means "the land where the sun rises." The area known as the Levant is bordered by the Mediterranean Sea to the west, the Arabian Desert to the north, Upper Mesopotamia to the east, and Egypt to the south. In ancient times, the Levant's physical location made it a bridge between Mesopotamia and Egypt. Southern Levant, also known as Canaan in the Bible, consists of modern-day Israel, Lebanon, and southern Syria. The culture of Canaan was influenced by dealings with Egypt, while the northern Levant, now northern Syria, was more influenced by Mesopotamia. As a result, the jewelry and decorative arts of the Levant are the result of an amalgam of societies.

According to scientists, settlements existed in the Levant from as far back as 10,000 B.C.E., when most humans were still primarily food gatherers. Archaeologists have found jade beads in the area that date back to 9000 B.C.E. By the Chalcolithic Period (4000–3200 B.C.E.), the people of the Levant were using copper; scientists have also discovered semiprecious jewelry components such as carnelian, turquoise, limestone, and hematite from this era.

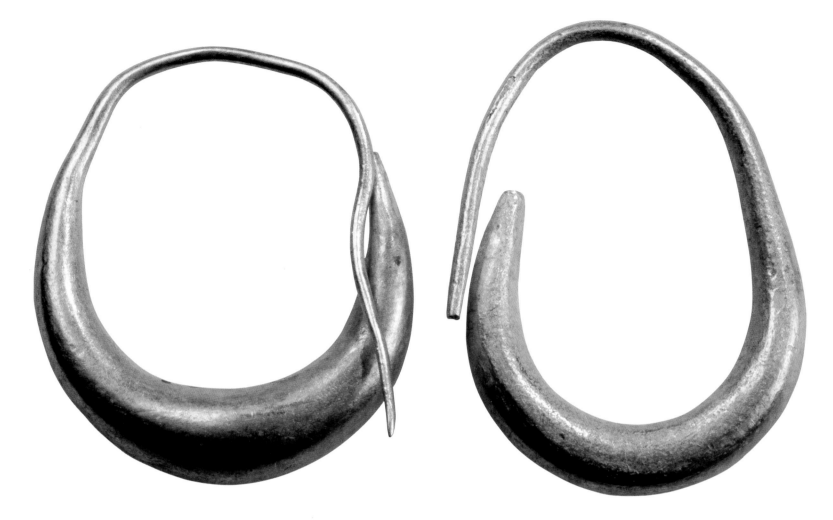

By the third millennium B.C.E., known as the Canaanite Period, the Levant was urbanized and actively trading with Egypt. This era, referred to by many historians as "the age of gold," saw a rise in Egypt's impact on the culture of Canaan. Because the Levant had limited resources, it imported gold from Egypt as well as from Arabia. In the Bible, Genesis 2:10–12 states: "And a river went out of Eden to water the garden; and from thence it was parted, and became into four heads.

The name of the first is Pison: that is it which compasseth the whole land of Havilah, where there is gold; And the gold of that land is good: there is bdellium and the onyx stone."

Canaan's culture evolved during the middle Bronze Age (2200–1500 B.C.E.), as the Semitic Hyksos (meaning "rulers of foreign countries") reigned over Egypt, bringing peace and prosperity to the region. One of the most important archaeological discoveries from this period

is the jewelry at Tel el-Ajjul near Gaza, where earrings, bracelets, and rings with Egyptian motifs were uncovered.

Lunate-shaped earrings were found in Mari and Ur and were widely distributed in Canaan during this period.

Pair of Lunate-Shaped Earrings
Deir el-Balah, 13th century B.C.E.
Gold
H: 2.3 cm
Gift of Jonathan Rosen, New York,
to American Friends of the Israel Museum
The Israel Museum, Jerusalem
IMJ 92.17.182

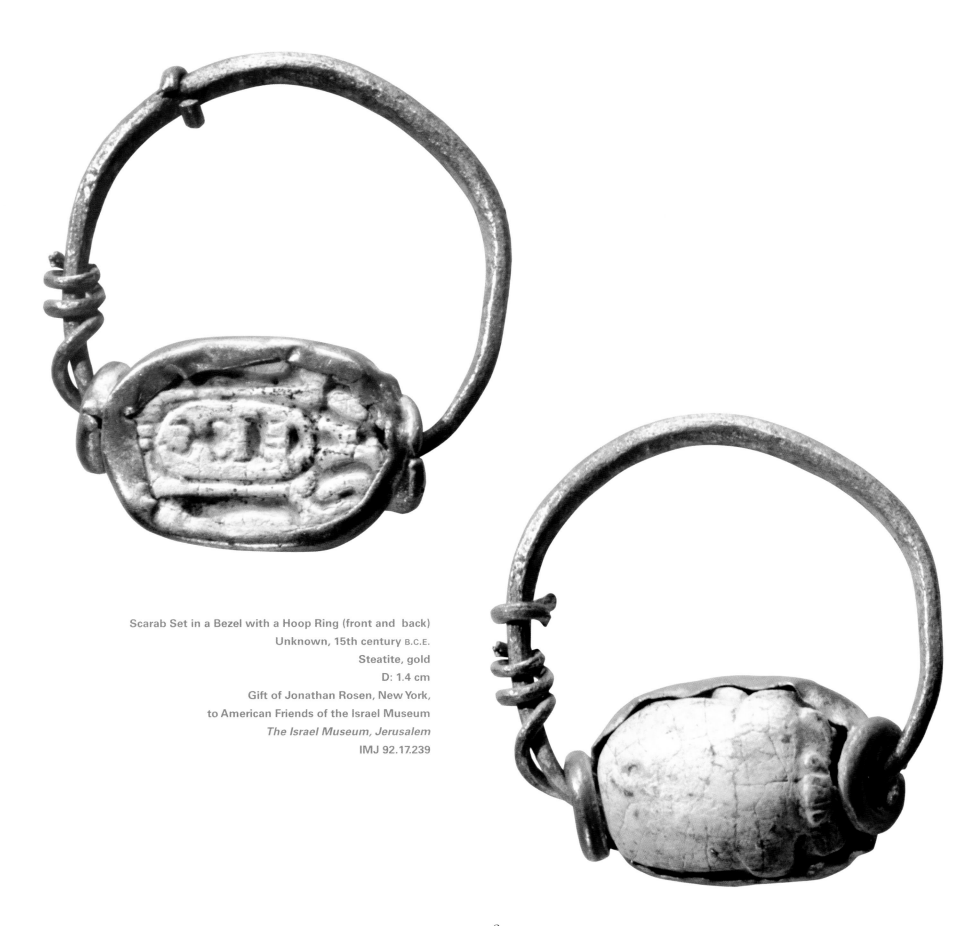

Scarab Set in a Bezel with a Hoop Ring (front and back)
Unknown, 15th century B.C.E.
Steatite, gold
D: 1.4 cm
Gift of Jonathan Rosen, New York,
to American Friends of the Israel Museum
The Israel Museum, Jerusalem
IMJ 92.17.239

One popular Egyptian design is the scarab ring, based on the image of the dung beetle, an Egyptian symbol of new life. The dung beetle rolls its dung into a hole where it serves as food not only for the adult beetles but also for the larvae. The larvae are laid on the mound and eventually they develop into new beetles. Egyptians associated this regenerative process with Ra, the creator god. To ward off evil, scarabs were worn by the living as well as the dead, regardless of social class.

The Egyptians introduced new jewelry techniques to artisans of the Levant. These new processes included *granulation*, in which gold or another metal is soldered with minute grains of gold to make a pattern, and *filigree*, in which gold or silver wires are twisted and curled to make a decorative pattern.

OSNAT MISCH-BRANDL

Osnat Misch-Brandl is the Curator of Chalcolithic and Canaanite periods at the Israel Museum in Jerusalem. She received her B.A. in archaeology and history and an M.A. in biblical and classical archaeology from the Hebrew University of Jerusalem. Mrs. Misch-Brandl has been a board member of the International Council of Museums and the Israel Exploration Society. She has authored several exhibition catalogs and has participated in excavation with the Hebrew University of Jerusalem in numerous locations in Cyprus and Israel, especially in the Timna Valley.

What is your area of expertise?

I am the Curator of Chalcolithic and Canaanite Periods at the Israel Museum in Jerusalem. The Chalcolithic period started around 4500 B.C.E. and lasted for one thousand years. It was a very long period—very mysterious and very wonderful. It was the beginning of the use of gold. In excavations in Nahal Qanah, eight gold ingots were found. It was also the beginning of the use of copper.

What were the gold ingots?

An ingot is a piece of metal from which you make jewelry or pieces that you want. The eight ingots were either solid gold or electrum, which cannot be used as rings for the fingers or arms because of their shape, so we assume that they were used for making jewelry. They were found in a huge stalagmite and stalactite cave some ten years ago. They were likely a burial gift. We assume that the man who was buried with these items was a distinguished personality in his community. Goldmines were found in southern Egypt and gold was imported to Israel already at that early period. This is the oldest gold found in the world—dating from 4500 B.C.E.—together with the pieces of jewelry that were found in the tombs in Varna, Bulgaria.

Did the ancients create jewelry out of this ingot gold?

We do not know exactly why they made the beautiful gold rings. They even worked the surface of the rings to make them shinier and brighter. It's hard to imagine what else they could have been used for.

When does the Canaanite period begin?

The Canaanite period is the period that follows the Chalcolithic period. From records that come from the archives of Mari, in northern Syria, we have the first mention of Canaan as a land. These records are from the second millennium B.C.E. From these archives, we have one tablet with cuneiform script mentioning Canaan as a country, as a place. Canaan means "land of the purple." That is the color that comes from mollusk shells. The name *Phoenician* means the same.

Where was the land of Canaan?

The land of Canaan was not precisely defined. We assume that the River Jordan was the eastern border; the Mediterranean the western border; Ugarit, in Syria, the northern border; and Beersheba in the Negev Desert, the southern border. That is quite a limited area, although in certain times it may have expanded.

Tell me about their dress and customs.

We know quite a lot about what they wore, not from local sources, but from Egyptian sources, such as reliefs showing the Canaanite traders coming to Egypt. They wore colorful and varied clothing and different ornaments. We have jewelry that was made in Canaan—not Egypt, not Syria, not Mesopotamia, although it was influenced by these peoples.

What are the characteristics of something that is typically Canaanite?

Pieces of jewelry from the cemetery near Deir el-Balah are very typical. Once you see them you cannot mistake them. Deir el-Balah is a place where you have a lot of Egyptian influence, but it was the Canaanites who made this jewelry. It's not the individual materials or the shapes, but the combination that makes it distinctly Canaanite. They used different kinds of techniques, like granulation, repoussé, and cloisonné. The cloisonné technique was used to create vivid and intricate patterns. It begins with a base metal, to which thin wires are attached, thereby creating *cloisons*, or separate areas enclosed by wire. For example, look at the necklace on page 56. The shapes of carnelian beads, known as poppy or lotus seeds, were typical in Egypt as well, but the combination of these beads—with the very long, folded, gold-leafed pieces and the spacer bearing the face of the Egyptian goddess Hathor—makes this jewel Canaanite.

Gold and silver were used everywhere, by everyone. Silver was less preserved and more expensive, as it had to be imported from long distances, such as Anatolia. Gold was a noble material and was mined in southern Egypt, not that far from Israel.

What about the piece shown on page 5?

This is an earring. We have parallels to this earring from Megiddo and from Tel el-Ajjul. Most of the beautiful jewelry comes from Tel el-Ajjul. Such a unique piece is not found anywhere but in Canaan. This earring was made in the cloisonné technique, and the empty spaces were filled with glass, which is now missing. Most typical is the head in the shape of a gazelle, where you see the horns, eyes, and mouth. This is a very typical Canaanite earring found only in Israel.

What sites reveal culture of the time?

An important site would be Arad in the south of Israel. Arad is a site from the early Canaanite period. In Arad, eighteen seasons of excavations were conducted by the Israel Museum. Today, you can see in Arad the wall that surrounded the city and even the large well from which people drew water some five thousand years ago. To the north you will reach Tel Lachish, which is also a very important city and which includes one of the most important sanctuaries from the late Canaanite period. Farther north is Megiddo, which is one of the biggest sites in Israel, where some of the most beautiful items were found.

By 1550 B.C.E. (the late Bronze Age), despite the Egyptian Pharaoh Ahmose's expulsion of the Semitic Hyksos, the Egyptians continued their interest in Canaan. The Pharaoh sent gold, jewelry, and ivory not only to Byblos, but to such Canaanite ports as Tyre and Sidon. Most Levantine jewelry of the late Bronze Age was made in Canaan but inspired by Egyptian culture.

The archaeological findings at Deir el-Balah, a burial site in Canaan, are evidence of the influence of the Egyptians on the Canaanites. Archeologists uncovered burial coffins as well as goods such as seals, pottery, and jewelry made of bronze, silver, copper, gold, and carnelian. These coffins, or sarcophagi, were typically two meters long and distinguished by two main features: exaggerated facial features sculpted in clay and hands crossed over the chests.

Anthropoid Coffin
Deir el-Balah, 13th century B.C.E.
Pottery
H: 192 cm, W: 62 cm
The Israel Museum, Jerusalem
IMJ 82.2.814

One important discovery by archaeologists was the finding of anthropoid burial coffins in Deir el-Balah with stylized faces, arms , and hands. Jewelry from this time was discovered inside.

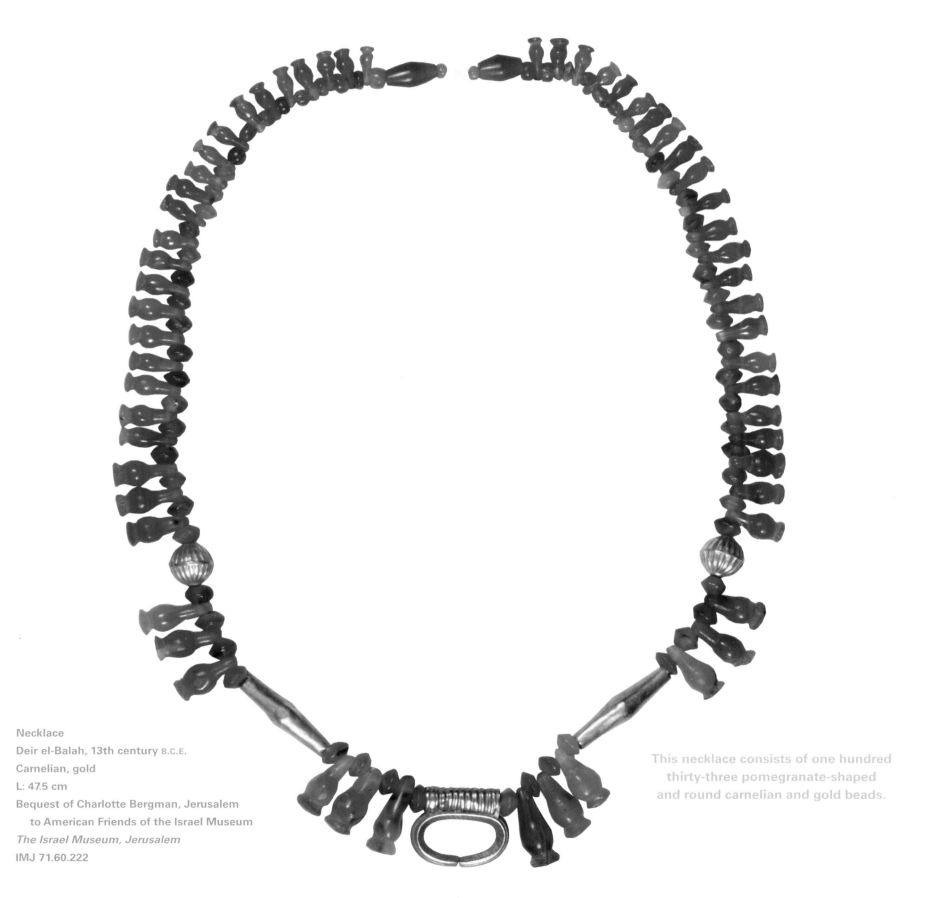

Necklace
Deir el-Balah, 13th century B.C.E.
Carnelian, gold
L: 47.5 cm
Bequest of Charlotte Bergman, Jerusalem
    to American Friends of the Israel Museum
The Israel Museum, Jerusalem
IMJ 71.60.222

This necklace consists of one hundred
thirty-three pomegranate-shaped
and round carnelian and gold beads.

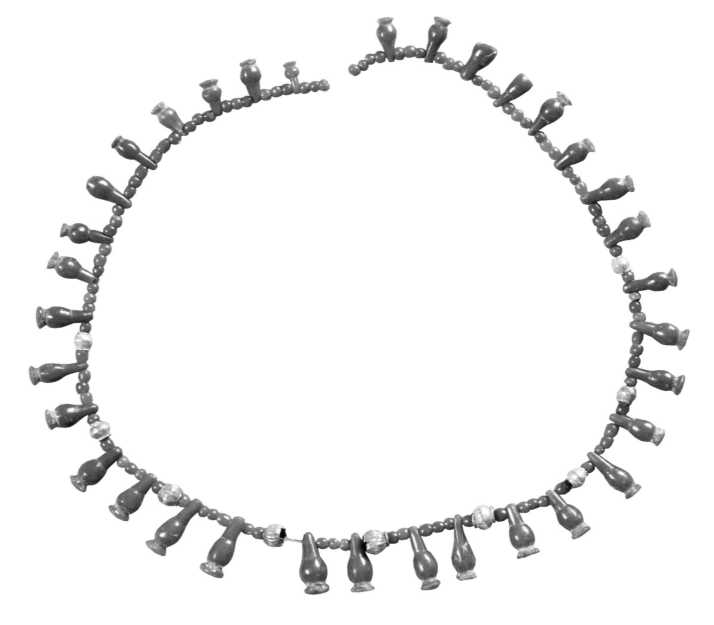

This necklace consists of one hundred forty
round and pomegranate-shaped carnelian
beads and round gold beads.

Necklace
Deir el-Balah, 13th century B.C.E.
Carnelian, gold
L: 46 cm
The Israel Museum, Jerusalem
IMJ 69.52.377

The gold and carnelian jewelry, also believed
to be from Deir el-Balah, shown on pages 53
and above, also exhibits Egyptian influence.
Carnelian, a member of the quartz family, is
brown in color in its natural state, and Egyptians
believed it had mystical powers. Egyptian tombs
were replete with such carnelian jewelry because
they believed the stone would assist with
passage into the next life. The carnelian and gold
necklace on page 56 is especially beautiful, not
only because the hand-carved blossom beads are
separated by gold spacers, but also because the
gold center of the necklace portrays the Egyptian goddess Hathor, the goddess of love and joy.

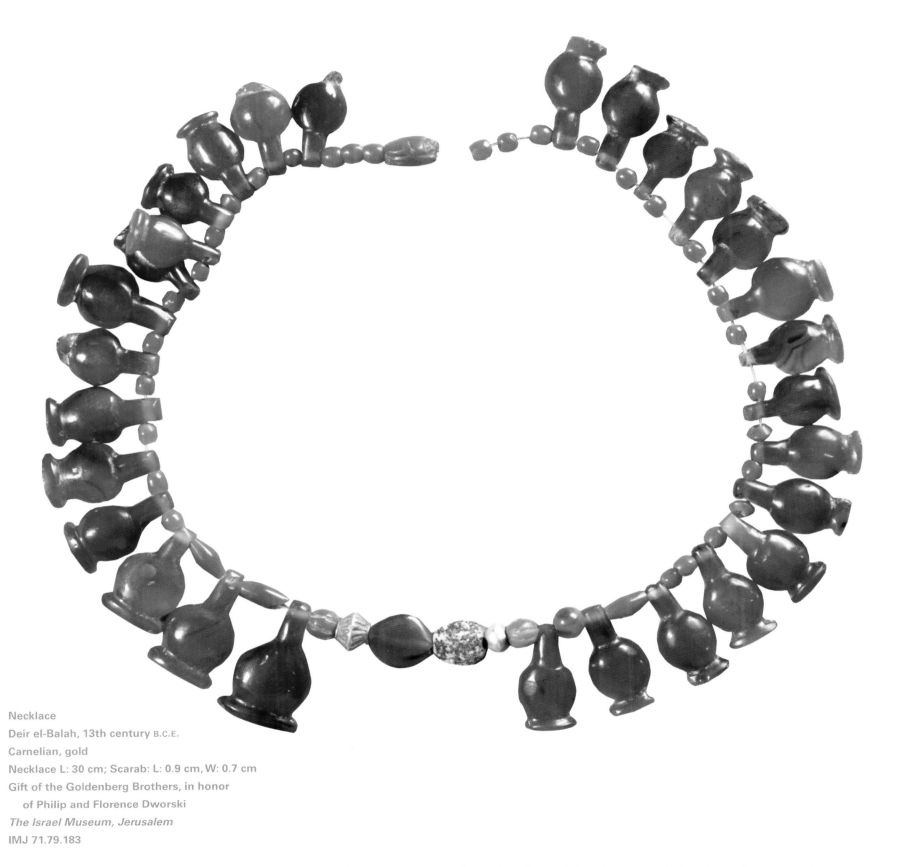

Necklace
Deir el-Balah, 13th century B.C.E.
Carnelian, gold
Necklace L: 30 cm; Scarab: L: 0.9 cm, W: 0.7 cm
Gift of the Goldenberg Brothers, in honor
    of Philip and Florence Dworski
The Israel Museum, Jerusalem
IMJ 71.79.183

This necklace consists of sixty-nine carnelian pomegranate-shaped and round beads, two gold beads, and one scarab.

Necklace
Deir el-Balah, 13th century B.C.E.
Carnelian, gold
L: 50 cm
Gift of Tamar and Teddy Kollek
The Israel Museum, Jerusalem
IMJ 90.87.426

This necklace consists of two hundred forty-four carnelian and gold beads and wedjat eye amulets. The center gold spacer is decorated in the repoussé technique; it depicts an image of the Egyptian goddess Hathor, the goddess of love and joy.

The shape of this amulet combines the human eye with the eye of the falcon, as it represents the falcon-god Horus. According to Egyptian mythology, the eye of Horus was a symbol of power.

Wedjat Eye Amulet
Deir el-Balah, 13th century B.C.E.
Red jasper
L: 2.4 cm, W: 1.6 cm
Bequest of Charlotte Bergman, Jerusalem,
    to American Friends of the Israel Museum
The Israel Museum, Jerusalem
IMJ 71.60.224

Pair of Earrings
Unknown, 14th to 13th century B.C.E.
Gold
D: 2.6 cm
Gift of Jonathan Rosen, New York,
    to American Friends of the Israel Museum
The Israel Museum, Jerusalem
IMJ 92.17.214

Pendant
Unknown, 14th to 13th century B.C.E.
Gold
H: 2.9 cm, W: 1.4 cm
Gift of Jonathan Rosen, New York, to American
    Friends of the Israel Museum
The Israel Museum, Jerusalem
IMJ 92.17.246

These gold earrings consist of eight gold wires soldered together.

Renée Dreyfus is Curator of Ancient Art and Interpretation at the Fine Arts Museums of San Francisco. She received her B.A. in philosophy from Boston University, her M.A. in ancient Mediterranean studies from Brandeis University; and her Ph.D. in Near Eastern studies at University of California at Berkeley. Dr. Dreyfus specializes in ancient Mediterranean art and archaeology with a keen interest in Near Eastern art and its interconnections with the Egyptian and classical worlds.

How did Egypt and Mesopotamia discover each other?

Commerce is always a good start—commerce and a sense of curiosity. Obviously, even in the ancient world people had to travel far and wide to fill their needs for materials, especially precious luxury materials, both worked and unworked, including gold, silver, electrum, carnelian, and lapis lazuli. Interconnections resulted from trade; the late fourth millennium B.C.E. was the dawn of an international age in which cultures learned much about each other and then went on their separate paths.

Along those separate paths can you explain the similarities or differences in their arts, their jewelry, and cultures?

It is easy to see the influence of Mesopotamia on Egypt during Egypt's Predynastic Age, before 3200 B.C.E. There are cylinder seals, similar iconography, fantastic animals—all of which originated in the Near East. Narmer's Palette, for example, is a slate with an image of this early king who ruled over the two lands of Egypt. On one side there are two long-necked feline figures with their necks intertwined. These are not realistic animals; they do not exist in the real world, nor are they anything you see in Egypt before this. They are composite creatures that originated in the Near East. On other Predynastic works there are images of an idealized king, much like the early depictions of the kings in Mesopotamia. There is a similarity in these civilizations, as they are facing much the same problems of administering large cities and ruling with the permission and sanction of their gods. At the same time, the administration of large temples, with their constant donations, also required management and leadership.

What are examples of enduring mythologies?

There are a number of mythologies from the ancient world that permeate throughout the Near East, Egypt, and the Old Testament. From the site of Ugarit, which is today's Ras Shamra in Syria, comes a legend about a king named Kret, who feared that his line would die out because his wife had left him and had to be brought back. She was the woman who had been promised to him to carry on his seed, his family line. He prayed to his god, El, who told him how to regain her. He then mustered an army (of three million men!) to accompany him to retrieve his intended bride. This sounds like the Helen of Troy story, which, of course, is the basis for the *Iliad* of Homer. According to one of my mentors, Cyrus H. Gordon, a similar story appears in the patriarchal narratives in the Old Testament, involving Sarah, the wife of Abraham, being taken from him two times. Both times Abraham must retrieve this woman who is destined to be his wife and carry on his lineage. So, it is easy to perceive a growing interconnectedness through these stories that intertwine eternally in the Mediterranean world.

What do you think is the significance of Mari is and what have we learned about it?

The site of Mari in wealthy, powerful northern Syrian illustrates the spread of the Fertile Crescent westward to the Mediterranean and even into Egypt. Mari was one of the outlying districts with strong ties to southern Mesopotamia, but these connections are not yet clear. What is known is that the extraordinary riches that have been found at the site, especially sculpture, decorative art, and jewelry, were amassed from Mari's close proximity to commercial trade routes that followed the Euphrates River; some passed through Mari and other overland routes began at Mari. The other important discovery at this site is the archive of cuneiform clay tablets. These tablets, found in a palace from the late third and early second millennium B.C.E., including over 2,000 letters, give us insight into the life of this city and its relations with other sites in Syria.

Why are you so intrigued by the Mari ivories and the Phoenician ivories discovered in Nimrud?

We all like gold and love to see the beautiful techniques that came about with the use of gold, but ivory was also a luxury material. Just think where it came from. You don't just go up to an elephant and ask for a tusk. Hence ivory was difficult to come by. The ancients loved ivory and it was a precious commodity, and at some periods in time, as precious as gold. Ivory was hoarded and was controlled mainly by the elite, the kings. The same way they controlled the gold market, they controlled the ivory market.

At various times during the last few hundred years there have been motifs of ancient arts becoming very popular—going in waves. Do you think we might see an emergence of another such period?

We never stop drawing from the ancient world for much of our architecture and our decorative arts. Think about the official buildings in Washington, for example; so many of them have the Greek temple as their inspiration. Rosettes, which originated in Mesopotamia, never seem to be out of favor in architecture, the decorative arts, and particularly in jewelry. Another eternal design is the Tree of Life, which also originated in Mesopotamia. Two animals flank a central tree, producing a formal, symmetrical pattern. I have recently seen firedogs from Marie-Antoinette's Petit Trianon that make use of this same design. Although the last time Egyptomania and a turn to Eastern motifs occurred was during the Art Deco movement in the 1920s, after the discovery of the tomb of Tutankhamen. These themes never really disappear; we are living with ancient imagery all the time.

Page 57 shows an eye-shaped red jasper amulet found at Deir el-Balah. It was originally set in a pendant and worn around the neck, presumably to ward off evil. Other discoveries at Deir el-Balah include the rounded scarab here and the square scarab on the opposite page. These faience scarabs were created with a jewelry process that was invented in Egypt around 3300 B.C.E., whereby quartz is pounded to make paste and then glazed to look like precious stone.

Egyptian influence is also evident in the pomegranate-shaped pendants on the facing page. Pomegranates are a traditional symbol of fertility because of the large number of seeds contained inside the fruit. Although the tree was not native to Egypt, King Thutmose I grew the plant and conducted botanical studies of it.

Scarab Set in a Bezel (front and back)
Deir el-Balah, 15th to 14th century B.C.E.
Steatite, gold
L: 1.8 cm, W: 1.3 cm
Gift of the Goldenberg Brothers in honor
   of Philip and Florence Dworski
The Israel Museum, Jerusalem
IMJ 71.79.187

In the Levant, scarabs were generally made out of gold and steatite.

Eight pendants formed in the shape of pomegranates, a common shape in the repertoire of late Canaanite jewelry. According to some historians, pomegranates were important in Jewish custom because the fruit's approximately 613 seeds represent the 613 commandments in the Torah. Some scholars even believe the pomegranate represents the Tree of Life in the Garden of Eden.

Pomegranate-Shaped Pendants
Unknown, 14th to 13th century B.C.E.
Gold
H: 2.3 cm (max.), W: 1.1 cm (max.)
Gift of Jonathan Rosen, New York,
   to American Friends of the Israel Museum
The Israel Museum, Jerusalem
IMJ 92.17.219

Scarab Set in a Bezel (front and back)
Deir el-Balah, 13th century B.C.E.
Steatite, gold
L: 1.7 cm, W: 1.2 cm
Gift of the Goldenberg Brothers in honor
of Philip and Florence Dworski
The Israel Museum, Jerusalem
IMJ 71.79.188

These earrings are made of eight twisted gold wires soldered together. There are eleven rows of tiny gold beads formed by granulation soldered onto the wires.

Pair of Earrings
Unknown, 14th to 13th century B.C.E.
Gold
H: 1.9 cm
Gift of Jonathan Rosen, New York,
   to American Friends of the Israel Museum
The Israel Museum, Jerusalem
IMJ 92.17.231

The center of each of these earrings is decorated with a grape cluster of five gold beads fused together using granulation.

Pair of Earrings
Unknown, 14th to 13th century B.C.E.
Gold
H: 2.5 cm
Gift of Jonathan Rosen, New York,
   to American Friends of the Israel Museum
The Israel Museum, Jerusalem
IMJ 92.17.235

One of Canaan's major industries was the production of wine. Hence we see the grape cluster motif on both pairs of gold earrings on the opposite page.

Another element common in jewelry from this time and place is the spacer, a device used as a decorative link in place of a necklace's regular beads. Six gold spacers are featured here.

Other jewelry from this period includes the two gold leaf rosettes, shown on the next page. These gold rosettes were sewn onto clothing, continuing a tradition that originated in Ur.

Around 1200 B.C.E. the mysterious "Sea People" unsuccessfully attempted to invade Egypt. Some say the Sea People were pirates, responsible for causing conflict in the Levant that lasted several decades. Nevertheless, the economy of the Levant was thrown into turmoil from which it did not recover until the ninth century B.C.E.

The purchase of jewelry resumed with the emergence of Phoenician trading. The Phoenicians from Canaan were called "Purple People" because they traded purple textile dye made from mollusk shells from Tyre. The three main Phoenician trading cities were Tyre, Byblos, and Sidon. Soon, the Levant was trading with everyone from Sicily to Spain.

The floral decoration on these spacers is made in repoussé in the form of papyrus bundles.

Spacers
Unknown, 14th to 13th century B.C.E.
Gold
H: 2.2–2.4 cm, W: 2.3–2.5 cm
Gold
Gift of Jonathan Rosen, New York, to American
    Friends of the Israel Museum
The Israel Museum, Jerusalem
IMJ 92.17.190-195

These rosettes are stamped in repoussé. The edges protrude
on the back, which indicates that these objects were sewn to
a garment or ribbon, a practice used during this time.

Appliqué
Unknown, 14th to 13th century B.C.E.
Gold
D: 6.2 cm
Gift of Jonathan Rosen, New York,
    to American Friends of the Israel Museum
The Israel Museum, Jerusalem
IMJ 92.17.202

Appliqué
Unknown, 14th to 13th century B.C.E.
Gold
D: 6.4 cm
Gift of Jonathan Rosen, New York,
    to American Friends of the Israel Museum
The Israel Museum, Jerusalem
IMJ 92.17.204

Ring
Unknown, 14th to 13th century B.C.E.
Gold
D: 2.1 cm
Gift of Jonathan Rosen, New York,
    to American Friends of the Israel Museum
The Israel Museum, Jerusalem
IMJ 92.17.228

Page 15 shows a Phoenician brooch with Spanish influence. This Tree of Life brooch has three little chains of the type later seen in Greek jewelry. The theme of life and the Garden of Eden, complete with goats and birds, is typical of the Phoenicians. One of the distinctive elements of this particular piece is the combination of granulation and repoussé, which is created by hammering the metal from behind to make the pattern stand out in front.

A group of objects shown on the next page features typical Phoenician jewelry of this period: lunate gold earrings adorned with a pendant knob, rings, hinged hoop bracelets, and an eye

The hoops are made of four separate coiled strips with braiding on top.
Perhaps they are meant to represent an unopened flower.

Pair of Drop-Shaped Earrings
Deir el-Balah, 13th century B.C.E.
Gold
L: 5 cm, W: 2 cm
Gift of the Goldenberg Brothers in honor of Philip and Florence Dworski
The Israel Museum, Jerusalem
IMJ 71.79.184

This large and impressive group of jewelry (44 various elements) would have been part of a hoard, probably buried as part of an individual's grave goods for safekeeping.

Group of Phoenician Jewelry
Phoenician, 7th century B.C.E.
Gold, blue glass paste
Private Collection

pendant made of gold and glass paste. Egyptian influence is notable in the bezels, or metal rims, of the rings and the eye pendant, which are modeled after the Egyptian symbol of the Eye of Horus, a protective amulet against evil.

In the late ninth to early eighth century B.C.E., the Assyrians defeated Syria and offered an ultimatum to the people of the Levant: either pay homage to the monarchy of the Assyrian Empire or resist and face its large army. The Phoenicians had no choice but to welcome the Assyrians; they paid tribute in gold, silver, ebony, and linen. In the Phoenician ivory relief shown here, we can see the influence of both the Assyrians and the Egyptians. At the palace of Ashurnasirpal II in Nimrud, excavated in the nineteenth century by Austin Henry Layard, historians learned more about these Phoenician ivories. Many of them were furniture inlays for magnificent thrones and chests. The relief shown here, which features a king plucking a flower from the sacred tree, most likely adorned a ceremonial couch. The style of carving has an Egyptian flavor; a similar relief can be found in the British Museum.

This is a beautiful example of Phoenician ivories used as inlays in Assyrian furniture. A similar plaque is on display in the British Museum.

Plaque with a King Holding a Sacred Tree
Phoenician, 9th to 8th century B.C.E.
Ivory
H with tangs: 9.2 cm, W: 5 cm
Partial gift of Emily Townsend Vermeule, and Cornelius Clarkson Vermeule III,
    in memory of Francis F. Adams Comstock
Princeton University Art Museum

PERSIA

Dress Pin with Head Decorated
with Floral Frieze and a Female Face
Luristan, circa 1000 to 800 B.C.E.
Bronze
H: 24 cm
The Israel Museum, Jerusalem
IMJ M 2026.66

Prior to the reign of Cyrus the Great, the Persians were just a group of Indo-European tribes. But with the founding of the Achaemenid Empire, Persia made its mark on the Ancient Near East. Beginning in 550 B.C.E., the Achaemenid dnasty brought prosperity and wealth to the Persian people that lasted for more than two hundred years. Cyrus' empire encompassed today's nations of Iran, Iraq, Jordan, Turkey, Pakistan, Israel, Lebanon, Syria, and Libya, plus parts of Egypt and central Asia—an expanse of 7.5 million square kilometers, nearly the size of the United States. It was the ancient world's largest empire until Alexander the Great conquered Persia in 331 B.C.E.

Geographically, Persia is separated from Mesopotamia by the Zagros Mountains, but trade intermingled the two cultures. In the southern province of Elam (today's southwestern Iran) was the cultural metropolis of Susa. Like its Mesopotamian neighbors, Elam boasted ziggurats, clay writing tablets, and the use of precious metals in sculpture and jewelry. Assyrians referred to these southern Iranian tribes as Persua. Since there is no letter *p* in Arabic, when the Muslims conquered Persia they referred to

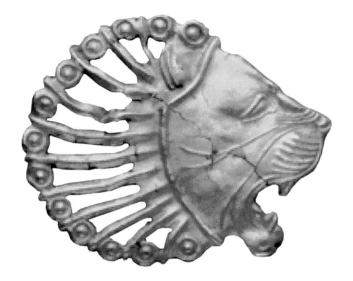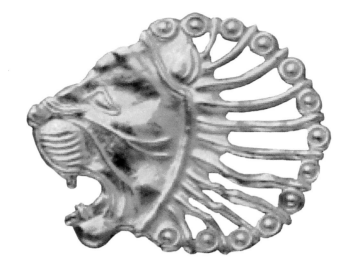

the people as *Fars* (hence the Farsi language). Another ancient Iranian tribe, the Medes, controlled the region to the north. When Cyrus the Great established a unified realm, including the Medes, it became the Achaemenid Persian Empire.

The court and its royal leadership enjoyed great prosperity during the Achaemenid dynasty. Gold and silver furniture, bowls, and cups were staples of the royal court. Every year the king would send lavish gifts to the men who produced the most sons; these objects were used as currency.

While much of Achaemenid jewelry has not survived, the pieces that did display wonderful inlays and playfulness in their themes. The most important find is the Oxus Treasure of more than 1,700 gold and silver objects, which depicts the influence of Mesopotamia and Elam on Persian jewelry. The Oxus Treasure takes its name from the Oxus River, now called the Amu Darya, which is one of the longest rivers in Central Asia.

Another great discovery comes from a water jar found buried under one of the pavilions at Pasargadae, forty kilometers northeast of Persepolis, the capital city that was founded by Cyrus. Over one thousand items were discovered inside the enormous jar, including bracelets, earrings, and a gold cloisonné button. Cloisonné is a type of decoration in which a band of gold is filled with enamel. It is believed that this process was brought to Persia from Egypt.

Here is a striking example of Achaemenid jewelry in the design of two lions' heads. The lion was a symbol of the king that was often used in bracelets and rings. These particular lions' heads probably originate from northwest Persia. They have a pierced openwork design called *ajouré* and are circular in shape. They were sewn into clothing, probably as amulets to ward off evil.

Lions' heads were a popular motif in Persian jewelry.

Pair of Openwork Bracteates in the form of Lions' Heads
Persia, Achaemenid, late 5th to 4th century B.C.E.
Gold
Each: H: 5.7 cm, W: 4.9 cm
Carl Otto von Kienbusch Memorial Collection Fund
Princeton University Art Museum

Because of the openwork, the lion's head would look different on every occasion, depending upon the color and texture of the fabric underneath it. As Dr. J. Michael Padgett, Princeton University Art Museum Curator of Ancient Art, explains, "Such lions are represented in museum collections around the world. They are pierced through the mane section to allow the fabric or leather on which they are sewn to show through. They could have been on a leather harness, or a robe, but they could also have been on tent hangings. The lion in particular is associated with the king of Persia—with his nobility and fierceness in war and hunting—and is related to the many earlier scenes of Assyrian kings going lion hunting. Whether they were actually stabbing them with a sword or throttling them with one hand is doubtful, but such images are expressions of their power. Being gold, the lions must have been special in their day; we may imagine hundreds of them, spangling the tent hangings and encrusting the magnificent robes of the Persian nobles."

Such royal imagery served as propaganda to

Animals were extremely popular during the Achaemenid period. They were portrayed with horns and without horns, in the shape of calves, rabbits, and rams.

Pendant in the Shape of Ram's Head
Achaemenid, 6th to 5th century B.C.E.
Gold
H: 1.2 cm
Gift of Jonathan Rosen, New York,
to American Friends of the Israel Museum
The Israel Museum, Jerusalem
IMJ 87.56.883

exert the authority of the kings who ruled an empire that stretched from the Aegean Sea to the plains of India. After the Battle of Salamis, the Greeks were astonished when they took the richly woven tent of Xerxes and with it the treasures it contained. In fact, the tent itself was reused to serve as a backdrop in the theater of Dionysus in Athens. The Persians influenced fashion in Greece as well, particularly theatrical costume. The Greeks were appalled by the ostentation and luxury of it all, but they were also enthralled.

Animal head bracelets decorated with filigree and granulation were a common type of Achaemenid jewelry; ibexes (wild mountain goats with massive, curved horns), lions, dragons, and ducks were all popular images. Shown here are duck head bracelets, both in silver. In the brick panels at Persepolis there is a delegation shown carrying bracelets with terminating griffin heads. Animal motifs also appear in earrings, like the gold calf-shaped one on the next page, and rings, like the exquisitely carved rabbit ring on page 73.

Pair of Bracelets with Zoomorphic Terminals
Achaemenid, 6th to 5th century B.C.E.
Silver
D: 5.2–5.3 cm
Purchased by Saidye Bronfman Endowment
    Fund for Archaeological Acquisitions
The Israel Museum, Jerusalem
IMJ 89.79.66

Pectorals, large pieces of jewelry attached by chains to cover the pectoral muscles or a part of the chest are another type of jewelry from this period. This adornment existed in Egypt before it became typical of Achaemenid artisans. The jewelry of the Persian Empire was a classical amalgamation of all the cultures the Persians controlled.

When Cyrus died in 530 B.C.E., he was succeeded by his son Cambyses. Nine years later, Cambyses' son, Darius I, took the throne. Darius quelled a rebellion of the Medes and Chaldeans, consolidated the empire, and divided it into independent parts called satrapies. Darius then moved the capital to Persepolis, the city founded by his grandfather. Persepolis blended the art and architecture of cultures from the region. Cedar beams came from Lebanon, silver from Egypt, ivory from Ethiopia, and gold from Turkey. Trade with the East was equally important for jewelry design, as exotic stones such as lapis lazuli and carnelian were brought to Persia.

In 331 B.C.E. Alexander the Great defeated the armies of the last Achaemenid king, Darius III, then marched into Persepolis and burned the city as a symbol of the end of the Achaemenid dynasty. According to Greek historian Diodorus Siculus, "Alexander described Persepolis to the Macedonians as the most hateful of the cities of Asia and gave it over to his soldiers to plunder. It was the richest city under the sun and the private houses had been furnished with every sort of wealth over the years. The Macedonians raced into it, slaughtering all the men whom they met and plundering the residences."

Eight years after defeating the Persians, Alexander himself died without leaving a successor. The generals divided up his empire, and Seleucus controlled the east; thus Persia became part of the Seleucid Empire, followed by the

Parthian Empire in 250 B.C.E. Art historians believe that the Seleucid Empire did not leave its mark on the decorative arts, but it was during the Parthian Empire that jewelry and the decorative arts experienced explosive growth. It was during this time that Persia developed the Silk Road, linking Persia with China and Central Asia. The Silk Road brought more than just silk; other elements previously unavailable to the Persians now arrived, such as precious stones, ivory, and metals.

Ring with Rabbit Head Motif
Achaemenid, 5th century B.C.E.
Gold
Private Collection

DR. JOHN MICHAEL PADGETT

J. Michael Padgett has been Curator of Ancient Art at the Princeton University Art Museum since 1992. He has a B.A. from the University of Kentucky, an M.A. from the University of Minnesota, and a Ph.D. from Harvard University. Dr. Padgett is a specialist in attic vase painting. Since 1996, he has participated in the Princeton University Archaeological Expedition to Polis Chrysochous, Cyprus.

The Phoenicians were reputed to be the greatest traders in the Middle East. Did their travels link the Mediterranean and the Ancient Near East cultures?

The Phoenicians were renowned as traders. They came into their own at the end of the second millennium B.C.E., when the Bronze Age civilizations of the eastern Mediterranean declined precipitately because of foreign invasions and migrations of people. This was the time when the Phoenicians, whose home cities were on the coast of Lebanon, west of Syria and north of Palestine and Israel, took to the sea and began to establish trading settlements not only in the eastern Mediterranean but in the central and western Mediterranean as well. In fact, they went all the way to the Atlantic Ocean and founded the city of Gades, modern Cádiz. They were a Punic people with their own Semitic language. Byblos, which is one of the great Phoenician cities, was known to the Old Kingdom Egyptians, with whom they traded. They were known locally as Canaanites, but as Phoenicians to foreigners. *Phoinix* means "crimson" in Greek, and this alludes to the famous Tyrian purple dye, which was one of their major luxury goods and exports. Another was cedar from Lebanon, which is mentioned in the Bible in the building of Solomon's temple.

The Phoenicians' archaeological signature is elusive, because wherever they settled, they did not try to move inland and establish agricultural settlements. This enabled them to have good relations with the native peoples where they settled. We do find purely Phoenician art in these places, but it is not as common as one might expect for so powerful and wealthy a people. In the Phoenician homeland itself, the archaeological excavations are hindered by the prevalence of the modern cities on top of the old ones, as for instance at Tyre. It is really by about 900 B.C.E. that we are able to recognize them archaeologically all the way into the western Mediterranean—in Spain, North Africa, and Italy. Sidon is mentioned by Homer in both the *Iliad* and the *Odyssey*, composed in the eighth century B.C.E. The Phoenicians were known as people who would take your goods to foreign markets and bring foreign goods to you.

The Phoenician traders were warriors as well. We find gold Phoenician inscriptions from Pyrgi, in Etruria, that allude to a treaty with a local king. The Phoenicians were everywhere along the sea coast, but they weren't there for conquests with massive armies. They did have a navy and were capable of protecting their own interests. In fact, when their homeland was taken finally by the Persians in the sixth century B.C.E., they thereafter formed the backbone of the Persian fleet in the Mediterranean. It was primarily against Phoenician warships that the Greeks were fighting at Salamis, Artemisium, and other sea battles with the Persians.

In the reverse direction, how did Greek travelers leave their mark on the ancient world?

The Greeks were always seafaring people, because so many of them were located on the islands and in coastal cities. Greece is mountainous, and although there are valleys and agricultural regions, you are never far from the sea. Even in the Bronze Age we have depictions of warships and trading ships. We have much evidence of trade that must have come from across the seas. The Minoan inhabitants of Crete were great traders. We deduce an increase in trade in the late eighth century B.C.E. as more oriental motifs come into Greek Art—sphinxes, goats nibbling the Tree of Life, palmettes, and lotus blossoms—designs and figures already well established in Anatolia, Mesopotamia, and the Levant. In the eighth century B.C.E., the Euboean Greeks founded a trade emporium at Al Mina in Syria, north of Lebanon, near the mouth of the Orontes River. Here they had direct access to Eastern markets. Several Greek cities traded there and left their distinctive mark. There was also a trading emporium of Ionian cities set up in the Nile Delta to access the North African and Egyptian markets. Egyptian raw materials came all the way up from sub-Saharan Africa: ivory, ebony, and gold. In the mid-eighth century B.C.E., the first Greek settlement in Italy

was established by Chalkis, in the Bay of Naples, at Pithecussae. The seventh century B.C.E. is what modern archaeologists often refer to as the Orientalizing period, because there is a greatly increased incidence of Eastern motifs in Greek art, such as the lions and sphinxes so common on Corinthian pottery and a turn to more floral ornamentation. The most important Eastern import to Greece was from the Phoenicians: the alphabet. The Canaanites wrote in cuneiform, whereas the Phoenicians developed a syllabic alphabet. This was adapted for Greek use, and then via the Etruscans and the Romans it comes down to us today. That is very much the most important Phoenician legacy, the letters we use and live with today.

What is the difference between the art of Ancient Greece and those of the earlier civilizations of the ancient world?

The farther back in Greek art you go, the more correspondence you will find, but Greece always adapted what it borrowed to its own purposes and transformed it into something distinctly Greek. For instance, the bronze cauldrons from Syria and Anatolia that had bull or griffin heads around the rims—you can tell the difference between the Eastern originals and the Greek versions pretty soon after the Greeks began copying them. In early Greek art there is a leanness and vivacity in the depiction of human figures that sets them apart. The Greeks not only traded with Egypt, but also served the pharaoh as mercenaries, leaving Greek inscriptions

on some famous monuments there. Of course, Egypt was full of colossal structures, five-story-tall seated kings, stupefying works of art—nothing like what you would find in Greece at that time. Greek traders and soldiers told stories of these things, and at the end of the seventh century B.C.E. we see the beginning of the line of *kouroi*, sculptures of young males. Endowed with good sculptural marble, Greek artists began to make figures in the same sort of rigid standing pose—one leg advanced, the hands down at the side. They are clearly based on Egyptian prototypes, but the *kouroi* are nude, which is not at all what you would find in the corresponding statues in Egypt. There is a different approach, not just in depicting the human body, but in the whole conception of humanity and ideals expressed in art. The Greek ideal of the youthful nude is the epitome of the inner virtues of man. The Greeks recognized this as one of the distinctions between themselves and Eastern peoples. When they captured the Persians in the Persian War and sold them at slave auctions, they found it hilarious that the Persians were embarrassed to be shown nude on the slave block, whereas this was commonplace in Greece.

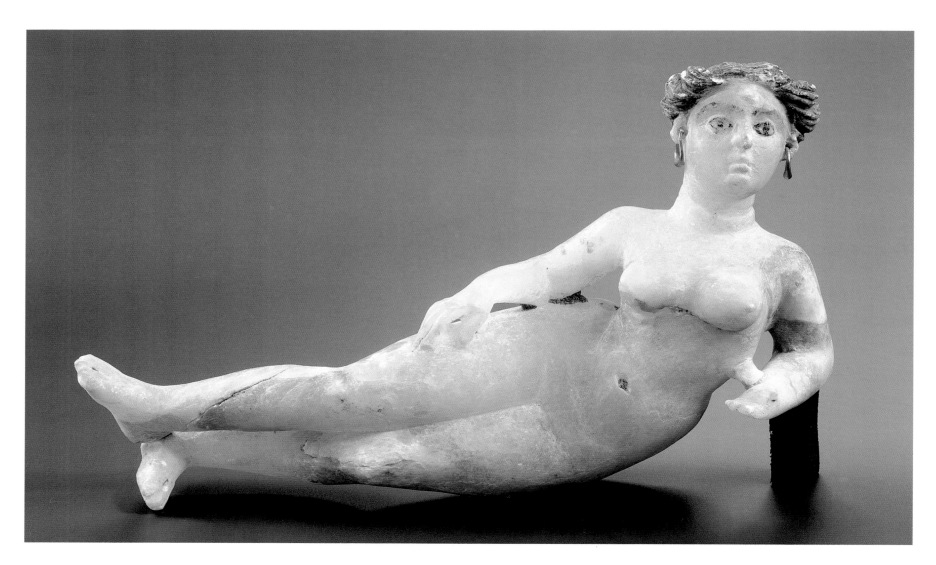

Figurative art in jewelry, especially images of gods and goddesses, were popular during this period, including representations of the Near Eastern goddess Ishtar (the goddess of fertility and war) in figurines linked to the fertility rite. Ishtar was one of the most important goddesses of the Ancient Near East. In addition to representing love and beauty, she was also the goddess of war because of her fierce sense of competition.

A stunning example of her representation is the Parthian statuette *The Great Goddess* shown above, depicting a reclining nude woman adorned with gold jewelry. She is carved from translucent alabaster with gold drop earrings. The earrings were most likely hammered and then applied to the figure. The Goddess has a voluptuous figure and is totally nude except for her jewelry. Reclining female nudes were foreign to the

Pair of Earrings
Parthian, 1st century B.C.E.
Gold, garnet, turquoise
H: 4 cm, W: 1.5 cm
Private Collection

The crescent moon was a symbol of Ishtar, the goddess of love.
We see this design in beautiful earrings of the Parthian Dynasty.

Ancient Near Eastern artistic tradition and were brought there by the Greeks. She is related to other Hellenistic female nudes, both in her realistic proportions and posture. Her physical features are Greek. The use of bitumen (a Near Eastern material created from asphalt, ashes, and plants) for her hair and her inlaid stone eyes identify an Eastern tradition. Her neck is marked with Rings of Venus, which are fleshy creases in the neck, a desirable attribute in the Hellenistic female sculpture.

Ishtar is associated with the lion and with the planet Venus. The crescent moon is also one of her symbols. A famous Parthian alabaster figure of her, now found in the Louvre, is adorned with an appliquéd gold crown in the shape of a crescent moon. This cresccent moon theme is also shown in the beautiful pair of Parthian gold and garnet ear pendants with turquoise shown above. This design, which influenced Hellenistic jewelry is composed of an inverted teardrop-shaped element hanging from a hinged earring. It is inlaid with a large cabochon-cut garnet surrounded by beads of gold granulation, with soldering at the wide end of the teardrop. The gold crescent moon is inlaid with a sliver of garnet, and a tiny turquoise pebble is set at the

Six bell-shaped pendants dangle from the lower half of each of these earrings. The bells make a pleasant tinkling sound when worn.

Pair of Earrings with Dangling Bells
Parthian, 3rd to 2nd century B.C.E.
Gold
H: 6.5 cm
Private Collection

The grape cluster is a motif that dates back to the third millennium B.C.E. and is seen on Near Eastern jewelry from the ancient civilization of Elam since at least the eighth century B.C.E.

Pair of Earrings in the Shape of Grape Clusters
Parthian, 2nd century B.C.E.
Gold
H: 6.6 cm
Private Collection

bottom of the pendant with a ring of fine granulation around the base.

In jewelry, Ishtar and her moon imagery are associated with spherical central pendants, as in the pair of Parthian gold ear pendants with dangling bells shown on the opposite page. These elaborately constructed earrings are made with a hinged strap hoop for insertion into the pierced earlobe. They are attached to an hourglass element with three granulated s-scroll straps from which hang a large, hollow spherical pendant. The sphere is made in two parts with six semicircles cut out of sheet wire to form the elements of the pendant. Beaded wire lines the edges and six flattened, bell-shaped pendants dangle from rings attached to the sphere's lower half, between the cutouts. The bells swing freely and make a tinkling sound as they knock against the central sphere and one another. These earrings might have been made for a dancer in the royal court.

Artisans of the Parthian Empire used the iconography of Dionysus, the Greek god of wine, on everything from jewelry to vessels. This Dionysian influence is evident in the pair of Parthian gold ear pendants in the shape of grape clusters shown on the opposite page. Most grape cluster earrings of the time measure from 4 to 5 centimeters in length, so these earrings, at 6.6 centimeters, are one of the longest examples ever discovered. The earrings are an excellent representation of the synthesis of Greek and Near Eastern elements that are indicative of Parthian culture. While the grape motif dates back to the third millennium B.C.E., the top of the cluster is fashioned in the shape of an amphora, a Greek vessel used for holding wine. The tapering cluster-shaped pendants hang from plain gold hoops; four arching handles made of beaded wire are symmetrically arranged around the shoulder of the cluster design to connect it to the neck of the amphora. Three vertically arranged areas of granulation, consisting of a triangle between two spheres, decorate each of the smooth areas of the shoulder between the handles. There is a small gold hoop at the end suggesting that there might have been an additional pendant element that hung from the grape cluster.

Typical of the period in the west of Persia from the 12th to 8th centuries were bronze objects such as this dress pin.

Dress Pin with Disc Head Depicting a Pair of Ibexes
Luristan, 1000 to 800 B.C.E.
Bronze
H: 22 cm, D: 8.3 cm
The Israel Museum, Jerusalem
IMJ M 5742.9.53

Pair of Earrings in the Shape of Nude Women
Parthian, 2nd to 1st century B.C.E.
Gold
H: 1.3 cm
Private Collection

The synthesis of Greek and Near Eastern design is also evident here in a pair of Parthian gold earrings in the shape of a nude woman. The head of the woman portrayed in the earrings recalls the maenads, the female followers of Dionysus; the youthful features depicted on the earrings are wonderfully detailed for their size. The enlarged, spherical face spirals are a Greek motif. As in Greek art from the eighth to the seventh century B.C.E., the exaggerated feminine form resembles a posture on a ship's prow.

During the third century B.C.E., citizens of Persia wanted to display their wealth; an example of this tendency can be seen on the opposite page, in the Parthian gold and garnet ring with an intaglio of a ruler or nobleman. The shape of the ring has Hellenistic origins, but the Parthian influence is found in the use of the large garnet cabochon, the ridged treatment of the central band, and the Persian dress. Unlike today's knuckle rings, which are worn on one to three knuckles by men and women, this Parthian ring was meant only for a man. It was worn over the

Ring with an Intaglio of a Ruler or Nobleman
Parthian, 2nd to 1st century B.C.E.
Gold, garnet
H: 2.5 cm, W: 3.1cm
Private Collection

first knuckle, preventing the finger from moving. The ring announces, "I do not have to work!"

The Parthian Empire came to an end in 224 C.E., when the last Arsacid king was defeated by Ardashir I and thus began the Sassanian Dynasty. This is considered one of the most influential periods in Persian history before the advent of Islam. The kings were patrons of philosophy, literature, music, and poetry. Paintings, sculpture, and pottery came into their prime. Sassanian textiles and rugs, influenced by Chinese silk weaving, were often sewn with jewelry.

Sassanian society was rigidly divided into four classes: nobles, priests, warriors, and commoners. At the center of society was the king, who ruled the nobles and the court, its household, and the court mausoleums. The king was celebrated by banquets, hunts, and different court ceremonies. These events became the most common themes in jewelry and the decorative arts. The king was shown on horseback, and his prey would include deer, bears, and lions.

A silver-gilt plate with a royal hunting scene is depicted on the next page. The royal hunt was a theme on Sassanian vessels dating back to the mid-fourth century C.E., but fine detail, such as the little finger of the bowstring hand bent downward, is not seen on plates produced before the fifth century C.E. The king wears all the ornaments of a royal for a hunt, including his crown and tight-fitting trousers and shoes. The horse is outfitted in elaborate gear, including an ornate saddle and bridle. As the hunt symbolized the strength of the king, this motif was popular on gifts for neighboring allies and rulers.

Hunts play a significant role in the Sassanian arts. This gilt plate depicts a royal hunting scene with the king, wearing all the insignia of a royal, sitting astride a horse.

Gilt Plate with Royal Hunting Ccene
Sassanian, 5th to 6th century C.E.
Silver
D: 22.2 cm
Private Collection

The richness of decoration on this beautiful bottle is indicative of the wealth and decadence of the Sassanian dynasty during its second Golden Era.

Gilt Bottle with Female Dancers
Sassanian, 6th century C.E.
Silver
H: 18 cm
Private Collection

A Sassanian silver-gilt bottle is depicted on the opposite page. This type of vessel seems to be more secular than religious. It was probably a luxurious bottle that decorated the table of important Sassanian dignitaries. The background is entirely gilded, while the dancers appear silvery. Links to Greek mythology are visible on this piece, with the four figures of nude dancing girls executed in repoussé. One is draped in spotted panther skins, holding a vase in one hand and a bunch of grapes in the other. These are attributes of Dionysus, the Greek god of wine.

Shown here is a Sassanian silver medallion that would have been soldered to the center of a silver plate or bowl. The style of this object shows the influence of Greek art on Persia. The medallion is hammered from a single thin sheet of silver, with the border and the monster's anatomy incised afterward. The figure depicted is known as the Angha, an enormous mythical

Gilt Medallion
Sassanian, 6th to 7th century C.E.
Silver
H: 5.6 cm
Private Collection

This striking medallion would have been soldered to the center of a silver plate or bowl. Traces of the medallion's original gilding are visible on the background outlining the mythical creature.

peacock-like bird with the head and claws of a lion. In legend, the animal is said to possess the wisdom of the ages. Since the animal preferred water, presumably the two spade-shaped forms to the right and below represent the closed buds of a lotus flower.

By 634 C.E., the head of the Muslim military command had wrestled most of Mesopotamia from the Persians. Finally, in 642 C.E. the great Arab victory came at Nahavand (150 kilometers south of Hamadan) and nine years later, in 651 C.E., the Sassanid dynasty ended with the murder of ruler Yazdegerd III at Merv. A new era was born. The Arab-Islamic dynasties—the Umayyads and the Abbasids—were the new rulers. However, other religions, such as Christianity, Judaism, and Buddhism, cohabited peacefully in Mesopotamia.

BYZANTIUM

In 306 C.E. Constantine the Great became the emperor of Rome. He ended persecutions of Christians with the Edict of Milan and eventually proclaimed himself a Christian. Twenty-four years later he made Constantinople the official second capital of his Roman Empire. In geographical terms of today's world, his empire stretched south from England to Spain in the west, across to Syria and Egypt in the southeast, and was bordered in the north by the Rhine and Danube Rivers. Constantine's great nemesis in the east was the Sassanian Dynasty of the Persians.

Constantinople's position as the second capital of the Roman Empire led it to influence all the arts, especially jewelry. Because the emperor accepted gold as offerings in the church, he built more and more churches and monasteries, decorating their ceilings with gold mosaics, fashioning silk robes with gold threads, and commissioning sacred ornaments made of gold. To ensure that gold and precious stones were symbols of the Emperor, laws were passed that prohibited the use of pearls, emeralds, and gold by those outside of the imperial household. The use of purple silk (used in imperial clothing) was also prohibited;

Ring
Byzantium, 6th to 7th century C.E.
Gold
D: 2.5 cm
Private Collection

84

Byzantine Gold Buckle
Asia Minor, 6th to 7th century C.E.
Gold
L: 5.9 cm
Private Collection

Pendant in the Shape of a Woman's Head
Byzantium, 5th century C.E.
Gold
L: 3.22 cm
Private Collection

punishments for the violation of these rules were fines as steep as one hundred pounds of gold or even death. Gold tableware and even gold chamber pots were prohibited. Exceptions to these rules were made only for jewelry for members of the emperor's court, women's jewelry, or for coins and dental fillings. For three hundred years, gold was the status symbol of the Byzantines, appearing on jewelry with religious symbols, including, after 450 C.E., the crucifix.

This page features a man's golden belt buckle, ornamented with a bird, that would have belonged to a member of the imperial court. This style of lyre-shaped buckle was quite popular until soon after the end of the seventh century. With Emperor Heraclius, who was crowned emperor in 609 C.E. and again in 610 C.E., men's clothing became tailored and adorned with elaborate jewelry that often featured religious symbols.

DR. BARBARA DEPPERT-LIPPITZ

Barbara Deppert-Lippitz is a leading expert in ancient jewelry and corresponding member of the German Archaelogical Institute. She received her Ph.D. from the University of Frankfurt. She has been publicly appointed as a certified expert for Classical art, and she is the author of two books, including *Ancient Gold Jewelry at the Dallas Museum of Art*.

When and why did the first Christian symbols emerge in Byzantium?

The first Christian symbols emerged in the mid-third century C.E., between 240 and 250. These were abbreviated representations of biblical scenes that are preserved in early Christian churches in Dura Europos and in other ancient towns in Syria. Symbols like the lamb, the Tree of Life, peacocks, or the monogram of Christ follow quite soon, but the cross as a Christian symbol becomes popular only in the fifth century after Christ.

Why do most of the objects from the early Byzantine Empire employ Christian symbols but use very little Jewish iconography?

The variety of Jewish symbols is limited. Occasionally, we find the menorah on objects. But we have to keep in mind that the Jewish communities in the various parts of the Byzantine Empire were comparatively small, even in Syria.

Does the earlier Egyptian influence survive?

The Egyptian influence on Near Eastern art ended with the arrival of Alexander the Great in Syria and the Levant in the late fourth century B.C.E., when the Near East became part of the Greek world. After Alexander's death, one of his generals founded the Hellenistic kingdom of the Seleucids in Syria, which lasted until the first century B.C.E., when it was turned into a province of the Roman Empire.

Why were many early Byzantine pieces made in Syrian workshops as opposed to other communities in the Levant?

Ancient Syria was part of what is generally called the Fertile Crescent, an area with excellent soil and good weather conditions. In antiquity, wealth and agriculture always went together. If you had enough food for you and your family, you could sell surplus food and buy other goods. Syria's agriculture was ruined at a later stage, but it remained strong throughout the Byzantine period. In addition to having strong agriculture, Syria also profited from the trade routes connecting the western and eastern parts of the known ancient world. Wealth always creates a demand for well-trained craftsmen, enabling these Byzantines to establish workshops. Byzantine goldsmiths in Syria continued a tradition of fine workmanship already established in Hellenistic times.

Were those workshops customizing bespoke pieces or mass-marketing their designs?

We know from literary sources that customers who commissioned a goldsmith gave him the necessary amount of gold. We can only assume that the customer knew what she or he wanted, or that they followed the craftsman's suggestions and advice. Sample books for jewelry might have existed. Silver-plate plaster models have been found. Mass production was restricted to simple objects in base metal.

Were marriage rings, depicting the profiles of couples, a Byzantine fashion?

Trends and fashions changed in antiquity, but more gradually than they do today. The marriage rings illustrate the subtle changes that affected even such a traditional shape. A first stage is represented by the busts of a couple either in a frontal view or facing each other. At a later stage the couple is standing with Christ or a cross between them.

Detailed scholarly research about Byzantine jewelry is still at an initial stage. Chronological details are difficult to establish, and different workshops are hard to identify. Most Byzantine jewelry is inter-regional, as the same styles, shapes, types, and decorative motifs occur in all parts of the Byzantine Empire. Similar or even near-identical pieces were made everywhere or were carried freely through the empire.

Who wore silver jewelry and who wore gold jewelry?

Whoever could afford it wore gold jewelry, preferably heavily encrusted with colored stones and pearls. Those who did not have the financial means for gold would wear silver or even bronze jewelry. Personal ornaments like diadems, earrings, necklaces, bracelets, and decorative finger rings were worn by women. Gold signet rings, belt buckles and ornaments, and fibula were made for men. A fibula is a brooch that held together the ends of an ancient cloak, a large piece of cloth that was wrapped around the body and fixed on one shoulder. Strictly speaking, neither a gold fibula nor gold belt fittings were personal ornaments, but rather status symbols indicating the social position of the owner. Another aspect of Byzantine gold work was fine amulets worn as pendants. Such ornaments played quite an important role during a period that was as superstitious as it was religious.

Do you think more people will recognize Byzantine jewelry?

Definitely. For the first time in the history of jewelry research, the British Museum organized a scholarly seminar on Byzantine jewelry in the summer of 2008. It follows a number of successful Byzantine art exhibitions that included jewelry in the last several years. A general interest in Byzantine art and history becomes obvious in the growing number of students studying and universities, like Oxford, teaching these subjects. More people are becoming aware that Byzantine works not only recall Christian traditions, but also represent an important period in the European history of art.

During early Byzantine times, both Christians and Jews considered Jerusalem to be the center of the Holy World. Christian motifs were an integral part of early Byzantine jewelry, and though Jewish iconography was extremely rare, it did exist. For example, most bread stamps of the time are in bronze and feature Christian motifs for making the holy bread for the Eucharist. However, the bronze bread stamp on this page features Jewish symbols. The bread stamp served to assert Jewish identity with such symbols as the seven-branched menorah, representing lamps of the Second Temple, which was destroyed by Romans in 70 C.E. The ram's horn, or shofar, is blown at the Temple to call in the New Year. The ceremonial palm branch, or lulav, is carried during the processions from Sukkat, the harvest festival that occurs five days after Yom Kippur, the day of atonement. The incense shovel is associated with the Temple's daily activities.

Today most Christians and Jews do not get married at home, but rather in a church or synagogue. During the early Byzantine period, the custom, which was inherited from the Romans, was to be married at home before a portrait of the emperor or an image of a divinity. The opposite page shows a sixth-century gold marriage ring. In contrast to marriage rings from two centuries earlier, when Roman rings were round and showed a profile of a couple who were often holding hands,

Jewish iconography was extremely rare in early Byzantine times. This bread stamp is cast with a menorah, shofar, lulav, and incense shovel.

Bread Stamp
Judaic, 4th to 5th century C.E.
Bronze
L: 5.5 cm, W: 4.2 cm
Private Collection

the newer Christian ring is square and engraved, with a cross between the frontal busts of a couple wearing marriage crowns. The groom is wearing a toga-like garment with a large brooch, called a fibula, at one side, and the bride is wearing pearl earrings and a pearl-encrusted collar.

Though the gold and niello octagonal ring shown on this page is not considered a marriage ring, it does contain wonderful Christian iconography. The niello inscription says "Because you alone, my God, have inhabited me with Hope." The bezel is engraved with "Lord, because you are God, save me." In the lower part of the ring, the Virgin Mary is surrounded by the twelve apostles as she looks upward where Christ is ascending into heaven. To create niello, silver, copper, and lead, along with fine grains of powder like sulfur or borax, are melted together. An object is carved and the niello mixture is applied to fill in the background of the engraved object. The completed object is then sanded and smoothed. This technique was also used by the Muslims and eventually raised the level of Islamic jewelry to new heights.

Marriage Ring
Byzantium, 6th century C.E.
Gold
D: 2.5 cm
Private Collection

Marriage rings were not part of the wedding ceremony as they are today. The couple in this ring is blessed, as indicated, by the bust of Christ above them and the Greek inscription that means "harmony of God."

Ring with Ascension of Christ
Byzantium, 6th to 7th century C.E.
Gold, niello
H: 2.5 cm, D: 2.1 cm
Private Collection

This ring was crafted with niello and features religious inscriptions. In spite of its small size, the upper part of the ring is the base for elaborate Christian iconography of the ascension of Christ.

89

Pair of Earrings with Peacocks
Byzantium, 7th century C.E.
Gold
L: 4.1 cm
Private Collection

Iconic status symbols were an extremely important element of Byzantine jewelry. A favored motif was the peacock, which wealthy individuals and nobles kept on the grounds of their estates to suggest a paradise like the Garden of Eden. Peacocks were also associated with immortality and renewal since their elaborate tail feathers regenerated each spring. The Byzantine gold earrings with peacocks, above, were popular throughout Byzantium and eventually the entire Islamic world. The earrings consist of a sheet of stamped and cut gold suspended from an arched wire. The engraved details depict peacocks on either side of a stand holding a decorated vase. A border of punched circles surrounded by wire frames the design. Five gold beads are evenly spaced and soldered to the outer edge.

Similar in shape are the Byzantine gold and pearl earrings shown opposite. These earrings were created with a floral motif of vines, leaves, and clusters, cut from sheet gold in a delicate openwork design. As with the peacock earrings, a wire border frames the design with a beaded outer edge.

The most characteristic jewelry technique of the Byzantine period was called *opus interrasile*, or "pierced work." Introduced around the fourth century C.E., the intricately chiseled gold was often combined with embossing, making the finished gold piece look extremely fluid. This technique can be seen in two fantastic pieces: an early Byzantine necklace with a cross pendant on page 92 and the openwork gold belt on page 93.

The necklace, with the exception of the small circular elements, is decorated with pierced work. It is composed of sixteen disks of two types: a design based on a hexagonal frame, containing an ornament of six acanthus leaves, and a quatrefoil leaf motif in a rhomboid frame. Acanthus leaf designs became popular in Greece during the fourth century B.C.E. and were integrated into Greek motifs, specifically in Corinthian columns.

These earrings represent a style that was very popular during the early Byzantine and Islamic worlds. The flower motif with vines, leaves, and clusters of grapes are cut from sheet gold in a delicate openwork design. The centers of the flowers are made up of small pearls.

Pair of Earrings
Byzantium, 6th century C.E.
Gold, pearls
H: 3.6 cm, W: 2.9 cm
Private Collection

Repoussé is used to indicate naturalistic details, and seed pearls surround each disk. There are two drop-shaped ornaments set with amethyst that resemble the disks. Eighteen circular elements (not using pierced work) have various color inlays. The cross pendant is composed of emeralds, pearls, and garnets. It is made in five parts, with a square in the center holding a pearl in a pronged claw. The pearls surrounding the outer edge of the cross are larger than those around the chain. The length of the chain and the size of the pendant indicate that the cross is a pectoral cross, meant to be worn on the center of the chest rather than just below the collarbone. Acanthus leaves are also the

This necklace is of the finest designs in early Byzantine jewelry. The elegance of the overall design, the sumptuousness, the choice of precious materials, and the various decorative techniques employed reflect the primary function of a personal ornament of that period as an expression of personal wealth and status.

Necklace with Cross Pendant
Byzantium, 6th to 7th century C.E.
Gold, oriental pearls, emerald, sapphire, garnet,
    spinel, amethyst, colored glass
L: 47.5 cm
Private Collection

Openwork Gold Belt
Byzantium, 6th to 7th century C.E.
Gold
L: 72 cm
Private Collection

This belt is decorated using the Roman *opus interrasile* technique of making patterns in sheet gold by cutting out portions of the metal.

Ring with a Cruciform Bezel
Byzantium, 6th century C.E.
Gold, garnet
D: 2.1 cm
Private Collection

The design of this cross, with repoussè figures and medallions at the ends, was popular, and it continued to be used into the 12th century. Christ is depicted wearing a colobium, a simple sleeveless linen robe from Roman times that came to symbolize humility before God. The colobium dates the cross to the 6th or 7th century, as later crosses favored Christ dressed in a loincloth.

Pectoral Cross
Byzantium, 6th to 7th century C.E.
Gold
H: 7.55 cm, W: 4.5 cm
Private Collection

predominant motif in the openwork gold belt. Each one of the twenty-four disks made from sheet gold has

six acanthus leaves. The disks are joined by hinges, and the belt ends as a three tear-drop pendant.

Another example of a pectoral cross is featured on the opposite page. While the design of the figures

is somewhat primitive, the central form of the crucified Christ is decorated with holy figures on the top,

bottom, and sides of the cross. The cross is made of hammered gold sheet with low relief outlines.

The back is plain.

This gold cross has a cabochon rock crystal set in gold in the center, unlike pieces from earlier times when rock crystal was used alone.

Cross
Byzantium, 600 C.E.
Gold, rock crystal
H: 6.9 cm
Private Collection

Leaf Pendant
Byzantium, 600 C.E.
Gold
H: 3.6 cm
Private Collection

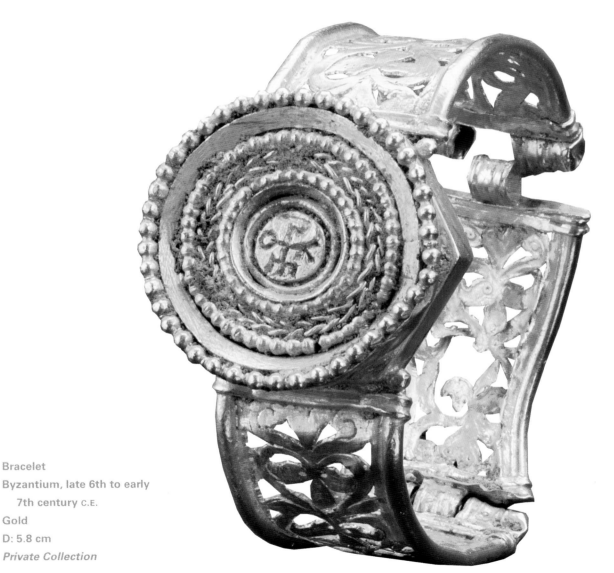

Bracelet
Byzantium, late 6th to early
   7th century C.E.
Gold
D: 5.8 cm
Private Collection

The cross on page 95 is set with cabochon rock crystal, suggesting the purity of Christ. The leaf-shaped pendant shown above is double-sided and was reportedly found with the cross.

Other trends came into fashion during the Byzantine era, including monograms and gold medallions. To the left is a man's gold bracelet with a monogram that reads: ϹЄΡΓΙΟV, "of Sergius." This monogrammed bracelet features concentric beading. The side is created from cut segments of heart-shaped leaves, and the bracelet is fastened by a gold screw.

Gold medallions were normally composed of two embossed gold disks attached at the back and encircled by a beaded border. An example of this is the medallion shown at the right. One side shows a standing figure holding a cornucopia, and the other shows a maenad, a consort of Dionysus, the Greek god of wine. The center is framed with vegetal scrolls, motifs often associated with immortality. Dionysus was a popular jewelry theme during the Parthian Empire and continued to be so throughout early Byzantine times.

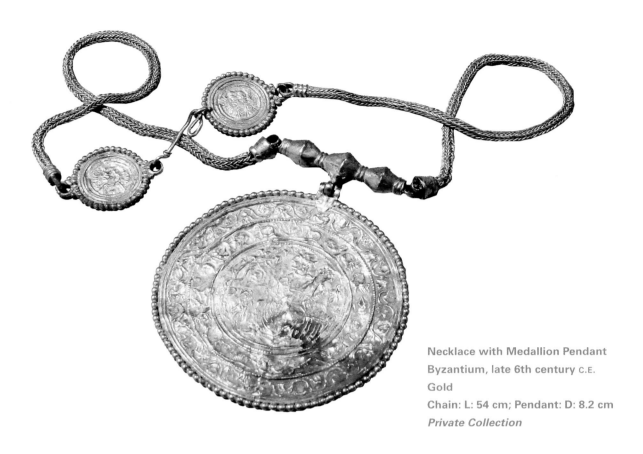

Necklace with Medallion Pendant
Byzantium, late 6th century C.E.
Gold
Chain: L: 54 cm; Pendant: D: 8.2 cm
Private Collection

Large circular pendants with figural scenes were very popular during the early Byzantine period.
Representations of Greek mythology, as in this piece, were as popular as religious references.

Front   Back

Plate with Dancing Satyr
and Maenad, Front of Plate
Byzantium, 565–578 C.E.
Silver
D: 25 cm
Private Collection

98

The bottom of the silver tray shown above has control marks stamped on it. These marks were used in the early Byzantine era to differentiate between workshops and to mark the weight and purity of silver. The front of the platter on the facing page shows a pair of dancers. The female, or maenad, wears a diadem with a medallion in her hair, as well as hoop earrings. The male, or satyr—although his face is wrinkled, his body is athletic—has a snake around his right leg. The dynamics of the dance are extraordinary. The frame surrounding the scene mimics the appearance of ribbon.

Five control marks are stamped on the foot of the plate, dating it to the reign of Justinian II (565–578). These marks distinguish the piece as a silver object of the highest order.

Plate with Dancing Satyr and Maenad,
   Foot of Plate
Byzantium, 565–578 C.E.
Silver
D: 25 cm
Private Collection

A *nomisma* was a coin weight equivalent to one-sixth of an ounce. Bronze and lead weights in various denominations were common throughout the Byzantine world.

Coin Weight with Pair of Imperial Busts
Constantinople, 6th to 7th century C.E.
Bronze
Private Collection

Bronze weights that were used to measure gold coins became decorative items from this period. The above image shows a small weight with a pair of imperial busts. The central figure, the archangel, is flanked by two busts, both wearing elaborate jewelry: crown, earrings, necklaces, and fibula (cloth fasteners). Greek crosses are above their heads, and the archangel has a star above his halo.

Other popular decorative objects of the period include bronze lamps and stands, like the one shown to the left. The handle of this lamp is very elaborate, and the cross, which is partially preserved, would have risen from between the two branches. The stand is likewise quite ornate, with tripod feet shaped like a stylized lion's foot.

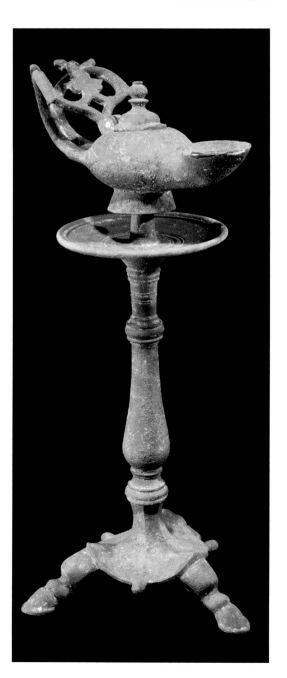

During the early Byzantine period, lamps were created in bronze and terra-cotta. This one is quite interesting because of its elaborately detailed handle.

Lamp and Stand
Byzantium, 6th to 7th century C.E.
Bronze
H: 36.5 cm
Private Collection

The prestige of the early Byzantine jewelers was so great that their styles and techniques were desired and copied by distant nations. According to one historian, a seventh century Byzantine necklace was even excavated from a Chinese royal grave. But the Byzantines and the Sassanians were in constant battle, and ultimately the Muslims were the beneficiaries. They were nomadic, highly mobile, and worked to convince nonbelievers to embrace their cause. Eventually they ruled side by side with Christians, but not without conflict that has endured across the centuries.

ISLAM

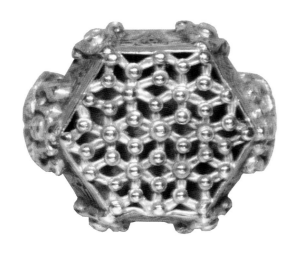

The belief in one god, and Muhammad as his prophet, unites Muslims around the world. Born in Mecca in approximately 570 C.E., Muhammad migrated to Medina in 622 C.E. This date now marks the beginning of the Islamic calendar. Muhammad did not see himself as a new prophet, but rather as one in a continuum of previous prophets that included Adam, Noah, Abraham, Moses, and Jesus. Like them, he believed in one god and was resolute in abolishing the idols that populated temples during the pre-Islamic period. After Muhammad's death in 632 C.E., his followers rapidly conquered Iran, Mesopotamia, the Levant, Egypt, and North Africa.

In the holy book of Islam, the Qur'an, jewelry is not directly cited, but according to some verses, precious materials, such as gold, pearls, coral, and rubies, are symbols of creation. However, later followers of the Prophet, whose sayings are collectively called the *hadith*, were more restrictive about adornment. Out of respect for Muhammad, Muslims remove their jewelry during prayer. The hadith also condemned goldsmiths; as a result, most goldsmiths were Jews. With this accommodation, jewelry could be bought and worn by Muslims, though they could not make it themselves.

This plaque, decorated against a niello background, depicts a lion walking.

Plaque
Iran, 12th to 13th century C.E.
Silver
H: 6 cm, L: 7.5 cm
Gift of A. Rabenou, Paris
The Israel Museum, Jerusalem
IMJ 3477.2.64

Can we detect any influences upon Islamic art from the ancient civilizations of Mesopotamia or Canaan?

There is no question that every new artistic language develops directly from what comes before, especially when we talk about a new religion, as in this case the Islamic faith that so quickly expanded from the central part of the Arabian Peninsula. They conquered everything from southern Spain all the way into northern India, encountering older civilizations in the area of the eastern Mediterranean and Iran. It is only fair to assume that, at the beginning, when they started to build and decorate their mosques and to create the first luxury items for their colleagues and the courts, they were calling upon the local artists.

Can you explain your observation that "the circle is everything?"

The circle can be intersected in many ways. Depending on how you divide it you can obtain a square, a triangle, a rectangle. And then you can intersect all of these. Almost every single pattern in Islamic art is based on the compass, derived from a circle. You start with circles and then create stars and an infinite number of combined shapes. The artists and calligraphers wanted to please God, because that was the ultimate purpose of these beautiful objects. So, the circle represents symbolically, in many ways, the perfection of God. The dot in the center represents the center of the universe, the place of God.

Can we detect the expansion of Islam into the Levant and into the West?

Islamic art was a passageway between the East and West—West being Europe and East being China and Southeast Asia. The Islamic world acted as an important trading region for many centuries. It was one of the main beneficiaries of the Silk Route and all the mercantile routes, including the Indian Ocean routes that were used to transport goods like spices. The Islamic merchants functioned as middlemen in these exchanges. They would develop artistic ideas in the various centers of Baghdad, Esfahan, and many other cities in the Islamic world, radiating both east and west. The interaction is especially obvious when we talk about the arts in southern Spain, where there was a strong input of Islamic art into the Christian art and the Jewish art of the same period. Another example is Norman Sicily, where Roger II, the newly arrived Norman Christian king from France, learned how to speak Arabic.

Stefano Carboni is the Curator of the Department of Islamic Art at the Metropolitan Museum of Art in New York. He received his Ph.D. in Islamic art and archaeology from the School of Oriental and African Studies at the University of London. He has served on the faculty at New York University, Hunter College, and Bard Graduate Center for Decorative Arts. Dr. Stefano is the author of several books and articles, and he has conducted lectures, seminars, and conferences around the world.

He loved Arabic/Islamic architecture, and he built his royal chapel with a ceiling that was decorated in the style of Fatimid or North African art.

One final example is how Venice, one of the European superpowers, adopted so much Arabic technology and artistic details, shapes, and design. The Metropolitan Museum exhibition entitled *Venice and the Islamic World 828–1797* demonstrated how, for nearly a millennium, Venice had very close contacts with the Middle East. At times, Venice participated in the Crusades, the European efforts to "liberate" the Islamic empires from the Muslims. But the city on the lagoon was also very pragmatic and lived on its ability to trade with the Middle East, for the Middle East was the intermediary through which the great riches—the silks, the spices—were coming from the Far East. Travelers had to deal with Middle Easterners in order to move these goods all around Europe. They did so by sending ambassadors to the main cities and establishing communities of merchants in Damascus, Beirut, Cairo, and Alexandria. The obvious result is an additional exchange of the arts and some culture.

What, in your opinion, is the greatest archaeological excavation of Islamic art?

The most important archaeological place excavated in the early part of the twentieth century is probably Samarra. The modern village of Samarra is about 100 kilometers north of Baghdad in Iraq, unfortunately today often in the news as a hot spot. Ancient Samarra was founded as the capital of the Abbasid caliphs, conceived as a great city but abandoned about fifty years later. The urban layout of the city extended for about fifty kilometers with its palaces, groves, hippodromes, and hunting areas. The ruins of the palaces are still visible, though crumbling and in very bad condition. The German archaeologist, Ernst Herzfeld, managed to record and describe the architectural decoration and paintings that were present in Samarra. It is the most mythical of places, but it is only in the past generation that archaeologist Alastair Northedge has been doing a proper job of professionally excavating and understanding the site, so its history is now much better recorded.

Were there diamonds in Islamic jewelry?

If we are speaking about Indian and Ottoman jewelry, objects include diamonds. However, the taste for stones in Islamic art, especially in later centuries in Ottoman Turkey, in Iran, and in India, is mostly for colored stones. Diamonds were only one part of a larger selection of stones. If we have the brilliant colorless diamond, then we need rubies, emeralds, and turquoise in order to make a very colorful combination. Diamonds never played the same role as today when a "diamond is forever."

What views about jewelry are expressed in the Qur'an or traditions of the prophet?

A lot of what we know about the life of Muhammad does not come from the Qur'an, but through the so-called *hadiths*, or traditions of the prophet. These are his sayings, or reports on what he did on a particular day. They were orally transmitted from generation to generation, then codified about two centuries after his death. So, the traditions of the Prophet, as much as they carry with them Muhammad's biography, are all subject to interpretation. A good Muslim believes in the Qur'an as well as the traditions, much as a good Christian believes in the Bible and its narrations. And, like the Bible, there seem to be conflicting opinions in the hadiths. For example, a common hadith relates that Muhammad said that gold and silver are only for materialistic people. So, silver and gold are not permitted on the body because it is an expression of secular wealth. Muhammad's teachings were followed within a religious environment, but this did not prevent the upper classes from making lavish use of gold and silver. It is true that there is not a large use of gold objects, and sometimes silver was considered even more rare than gold. Very few silver and gold objects survive from the Islamic period, but this could be because they were often reused to make coins. On the other hand, this may result from a tradition: when the caliph ordered a new Qur'an, plenty of gold was used to illuminate it. In fact, as far as we know, the caliphs and the sultans might have worn heavy jewelry and ten rings on their fingers because they wanted to show off their wealth and power and emulate the Byzantine or Chinese emperor.

This necklace consists of fourteen hollow gold beads and fourteen glass beads, which are crumb-decorated. The contrast between the gold and glass beads is striking.

Necklace
Iran, 6th to 8th century C.E.
Gold, glass
L: 62 cm
The Israel Museum, Jerusalem
IMJ 74.49.253

Few examples of early Islamic jewelry from the eighth century C.E. remain intact. Since the Muslims did not bury jewelry with their dead, very little early Islamic jewelry has survived. Gold or silver was generally melted down and stones were often restrung. Surviving pieces from this early period express Byzantine, Roman, and Persian motifs. It was not until the eleventh century C.E. that Islamic jewelry came into its own. The gold and glass bead necklace shown above is more reminiscent of early Byzantine jewelry than typical Islamic jewelry.

From the eleventh through the thirteenth centuries C.E., granulation and filigree were the most important Islamic jewelry techniques. An excellent example of both techniques is the gold armlet on the opposite page, which dates to the first half of the eleventh century. In this armlet, there are four hemispheres surrounding the clasp. The flat disks on the backs of these four hemispheres are decorated with imprints of coins, a style reminiscent of early Byzantine jewelry, which often incorporated coins. On the coins, the Arabic inscription reads: "Justice! There is no god save Allah, and he has no associate. Al-Kadir billah." The bracelet's twisted shank evokes the spirit of Greek jewelry. This armlet is missing stones, but a virtually identical bracelet, adorned with four turquoise stones on each globe, resides at the Frier Gallery in Washington, D.C.

Filigree and granulation techniques are also used in the eleventh century gold roundel from Iran on the next page. At first glance, the roundel resembles Fatimid style. The Fatimid Dynasty prevailed from 909 C.E. to 1171 C.E. It was founded by Said ibn Husayn of Syria and named after Fatimah, the daughter of the prophet Muhammad. Fatimid jewelry is more elaborate than filigree; if this piece was constructed in Fatimid style, the strips on the back of the gold piece (not shown) would be thicker and vary in size. However, the strips in this piece are thinner and are arranged in a regular pattern, indicating that it is not, in fact, a Fatimid. The roundel, which is missing a stone in the middle, has tiny holes in the points of the design, so it was

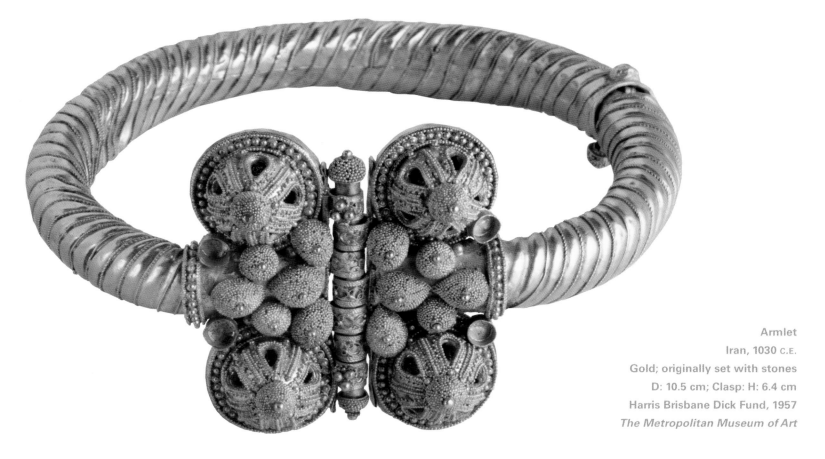

Armlet
Iran, 1030 C.E.
Gold; originally set with stones
D: 10.5 cm; Clasp: H: 6.4 cm
Harris Brisbane Dick Fund, 1957
The Metropolitan Museum of Art

From the 11th to the 13th centuries, granulation and filigree were techniques frequently used in Islamic jewelry. Both techniques are displayed in exquisite armlet and roundel objects.

Roundel
Iran, 11th century C.E.
Gold; originally set with stone
D: 7.1 cm
The Alice and Nasli Heeramaneck Collection, 1980
The Metropolitan Museum of Art

probably meant to be sewn onto clothing, similar to the Achaemenid lions' heads on page 69.

An example of a Fatimid piece can be seen here. This gold pendant dates to the eleventh century C.E. Its filigree designs are composed of many sections of gold ribbon curled in the shape of figure-eights, then soldered within a half moon–shaped framework of twisted gold wire. Beads of granulation decorate the outer curve of the pendant. Within the central circular section, framed by twisted wire, ribbons of gold have been arranged to spell out the name of the prophet Muhammad in Arabic. The spaces between and within the letters are filled with looped ribbon, camouflaging the inscription within the overall design of the piece. The crescent shape is often used as a design element in Islamic art.

The gold bracelet on the next page, from twelfth century Iran, is constructed solely of sheet gold, worked in repoussé (a technique for creating relief in gold). Granulation and bitumen highlight the decoration, with a conical glazed quartz held in place by four prongs. The bracelet is now set with a pink sapphire and

This beautifully designed pendant is composed of ribbons of gold. The name of the prophet is spelled out in Arabic.

Pendant
Islamic, 11th century C.E.
Gold
L: 3.2 cm
Private Collection

This bracelet was created from tubular sheet construction with repouseé decorations.

Bracelet
Iran, 12th century C.E.
Gold, glazed quartz, ruby, garnet
D: 7.6 cm (max.)
Harris Brisbane Dick Fund, 1959
The Metropolitan Museum of Art

garnet, but it originally contained two different stones. There are others that exist that are similar in spirit to the sheet gold bracelet. Impressively, silver granulation was used on some of these objects; this effect is harder to achieve with silver, because silver becomes less pliable and therefore more brittle with repeated heating.

A fantastic Islamic necklace on the opposite page raises the art of granulation and geometry to a new level. Each of the twenty-three granu-lated balls is a perfect twelve-sided polygon with a circle in the center of each side, transforming the necklace into a modern image. Many Islamic necklaces are comprised of twenty-three beads, but according to experts there is no known significance to the number twenty-three. However, thirty-three, sixty-six, and particularly ninety-nine are significant numbers in Islam because they are based on the ninety-nine names of Allah or fractions thereof. Many *tasbíhs* (prayer beads) possess this number of beads.

Necklace
Iran, 11th to 12th century C.E.
Gold
D of each bead: 1.3 cm
Hess Foundation Gift, 1972
The Metropolitan Museum of Art

The emphasis of this Islamic necklace is strictly on the importance of the geometric shape.
Granulation is raised to new heights and, although the necklace is ten centuries old, the effect is timeless.

This pendant is similar in design to the earrings on the opposite page. Nature continued to play an important role in jewelry design.

Pendant
Greater Iran, 11th to 12th century C.E.
Gold
D: 5.9 cm (max.)
Shamina Talyarkhar Gift, 2007
The Metropolitan Museum of Art

Other themes concerning jewelry emerge from studying the Qur'an. Because of the prohibition on the representation of a human form, figurative jewelry does not exist. As a result, the basis of Islamic jewelry is a combination of mathematics (geometry), calligraphy, and floral patterns. Calligraphy is especially prominent in men's signet rings.

Nature and the Garden of Eden also play important roles in Islam and the Qur'an. Birds, often peacocks, are central themes. The earrings and pendant shown above and on the previous page demonstrate this source of inspiration. The kissing birds of paradise are created in exacting detail, with granulating and twisted wire filigree reminiscent of Sassanian designs. Each earring has a crescent-shaped body created as a box construction on the top and bottom. Stripes of gold with granulation at the edges hold two openwork filigree bands on the sides, each containing a row of ten small decorative medallions. The two birds stand on tiny feet in the

The Garden of Eden continues to play an important role in Islamic jewelry, with birds being a central theme. Here we see two delicate pairs of birds, touching at their beaks and chests as they stand on their tiny feet in the middle of the crescents.

Pair of Earrings
Greater Iran, 11th to 12th century C.E.
Gold
W: 6.1 cm
Friends of the Islamic Art and Harvey and
    Elizabeth Plotnick Gift, 2006
The Metropolitan Museum of Art

middle of each crescent. Their bodies, wings, and necks are done in filigree, and their heads are formed from gold sheet with granulation on the surface. Seven prongs, formed by a short stem and a rather large cap decorated with granulation, protrude from the lower strip at regular intervals; five additional identical prongs extend diagonally from the exterior openwork band, corresponding to the outer and more visible side of each earring. The stems of the prongs are pierced, suggesting that strings of pearls were once used to decorate these objects.

Animal motifs are also evident in the goat figurine shown here and animal earrings on the opposite page. From the same period are two gold hair ornaments with a bronze core on page 116. They are fabricated from sheets of gold, decorated with twisted wire, granulation, and originally colored cloth. Each ornament was worn

Goat Figurine
Iran, 12th to 13th century C.E.
Gold
H: 10.5 cm, L: 10.5 cm
Bequest of Anna Ternbach, New York
The Israel Museum, Jerusalem
IMJ 97.95.28

The body of the goat was formed from two parts that were later joined together. The ears, horns, and tail were produced separately and attached to the body. The major decorative element is twisted wire, which is applied in small circles placed closely together on the body. This particular decorative style is characteristic of gold Seljuk jewelry from Iran.

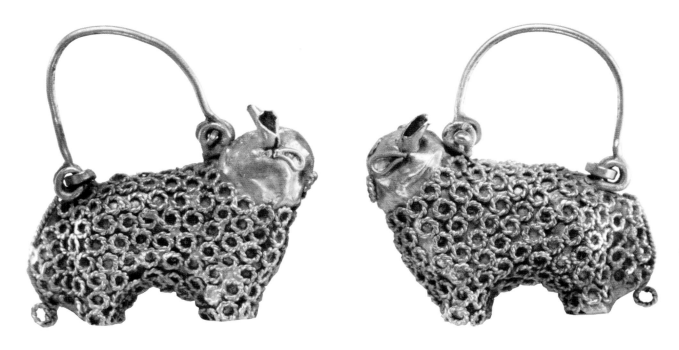

Pair of Earrings
Iran, 12th century c.e.
Gold
H: 4 cm, L: 4 cm
Gift of Tamar and Teddy Kollek, Jerusalem
The Israel Museum, Jerusalem
IMJ 90.87.433

This pair of feline-shaped earrings was formed from two parts that were soldered together. This pair is decorated similarly to the goat on the opposite page. Earrings in the form of animals were very popular in Iran during the Seljuk period.

Single Lion-Shaped Earring
Iran, 12th century c.e.
Gold
H: 4 cm, L: 4 cm
Gift of Tamar and Teddy Kollek, Jerusalem
The Israel Museum, Jerusalem
IMJ 91.103.371

This earring is in the shape of a lion; its body was formed in two parts that were soldered together. The head, ears, feet, and tail were produced separately and joined to it. It is decorated with twisted wire fashioned into closely packed rings.

Although hair ornaments were discovered as early as 2500 B.C.E., here is a pair of Islamic hair ornaments with emphasis on the geometric core.

Hair Ornaments
Iran, 12th to 13th century C.E.
Gold, bronze core, and originally, colored cloth
H: (left) 7 cm, (right) 7.3 cm W: 2.1 cm
Rogers Fund, 1952
The Metropolitan Museum of Art

around a long lock of hair. Hair ornaments were typical of Mesopotamia, and have also been discovered at Ur dating from as early as 2500 B.C.E.

During the twelfth through fourteenth centuries C.E., the middle class, especially in Iran, desired new and artistic metal objects to demonstrate their position and status. These objects were covered with niello, a metallic alloy used to fill in depressions that was originally developed by the Egyptians.

Above features an inkwell carved with faces, and the calligraphy inscription reads "Continuing glory, increasing prosperity, secure life, and good fortune." The top and bottom bands of the inkwell have twelve eight-lobed medallions containing the signs of the zodiac set in

The excellent state of preservation makes this inkwell one of the best surviving examples of its kind. Between two bands of quadrupeds are the twelve signs of the Zodiac set in eight-pointed stars.

Inkwell with Lid
Iran, early 13th century C.E.
Brass, inlaid with silver
H with lid: 14.9 cm, D: 11.5cm
Harris Brisbane Dick Fund, 1959
The Metropolitan Museum of Art

Casket
Iran, mid-13th century C.E.
Brass, inlaid with silver
H: 14 cm; W: 14 cm
Edward C. Moore Collection, 1891
The Metropolitan Museum of Art

eight-pointed stars. Inside the cover are human faces, with five medallions in between, each containing one or two birds.

Like the inkwell, the casket above has a beautifully detailed surface reminiscent of Sassanian metal traditions. The shape of this metal box—rectangular, with slightly tapering walls and a cover—was common during the

thirteenth century C.E. The four sides are covered with scrolls. A frieze of animals rings the top and base of the casket. In the center is a seated figure, and on either side are two kneeling attendants; the same figure reappears on the roof of the casket and on both ends.

During this period, rings were worn by both men and women. Men's rings also served as seals and often had the name of the owner engraved in calligraphy on the back of the bezel. The silver ring on page 16 and the lapis lazuli ring shown here are two examples of early Islamic finger rings. One, in silver, has a carnelian intaglio set in a fabricated pie-dish bezel with notched shoulders. There is a two-line inscription, written in the negative, in Kufic, Islam's oldest form of calligraphy. The other ring, in gold, is set with lapis lazuli in a conical box setting. The inscription reads, "God sufficeth me," a phrase from the Qur'an.

On page 9 is a flat gold finger ring with an engraved green jasper intaglio. A fantastic gold finger ring shown to the right, with a flat carnelian intaglio, has the names of Muhammad and the twelve Shī'a imāms engraved on it. The upper and lower sections of each prong are decorated with engraved hatching and fleur-de-lis designs. The spaces between the prongs are also decorated with bands of engraved hatching and floral scrolls with niello. The shoulders of the ring are engraved with floral designs and highlighted with niello.

Ring
Middle East, 9th to 10th century C.E.
Gold, lapis lazuli
H: 19 mm
Private Collection

The lapis lazuli intaglio is engraved with a two-line Kufic inscription, "Allah," and "God sufficeth me."

Seal ring
Middle East, 13th century C.E.
Gold, carnelian
H: 18 mm
Private Collection

This ring has a rectangular bezel set with a flat carnelian intaglio. It is engraved with a three-line Kufic inscription that gives the names of the twelve Shī'a imāms.

Fatimid designs were stylized and very ornate. These rings are fabricated from gold sheet, filigree, and granulation that were used to decorate them with scrolls and rosettes.

Ring
Fatimid, late 10th century C.E.
Gold
H: 24 mm
Private Collection

Ring
Fatimid, mid-11th century C.E.
Gold
H: 24 mm
Private Collection

The late tenth century C.E. Fatimid gold finger ring above is fabricated from sheet gold. The top of the flat oval bezel is made separately of filigree wire and granulation soldered to the medallion. A more elaborate Fatimid ring from the mid-eleventh century is also shown here. It has a flat hexagonal bezel that is decorated within an applied wire border with a six-petal rosette of six applied wires. Surrounding the rosette is granulation of varying sizes.

A Seljuq dynasty gold finger ring in the shape of a stirrup is featured on the opposite page. The Seljuqs were a Sunni Muslim Dynasty that ruled the Middle East and Central Asia from the eleventh to the fourteenth century C.E. In this ring, a cabochon malachite is held in place by fourteen tip-pointed, wedge-shaped prongs soldered against the high bezel. The sides of the ring are finely engraved.

This ring has a bezel set with a cabochon malachite gem.

Ring in Shape of Stirrup
Middle East, 13th to 14th century C.E.
Gold, malachite
H: 26 mm
Private Collection

This ring has a raised round bezel set with black jasper. It is engraved in cursive script with thick shafts like trees. The inscription reads: "He who guides towards the good is enough [reward] for the good."

Ring
Middle East, 18th century C.E.
Gold, black jasper
H: 28 mm
Private Collection

The seal stone bears an inscription in cursive Arabic in reverse, and the bezel is decorated on all sides with a band of Arabic inscription against a niello background.

Seal Ring
Iran, 12th to 13th century
Gilded silver, carnelian
H: 2 cm, D: 2 cm
The Israel Museum, Jerusalem
IMJ O.S. 2245.66

This signet ring is engraved on both the bezel and the seal.

Ring
Iran, 15th to early 16th century C.E.
Gold, nephrite sealstone
H: 3.5 cm, D: 2.5 cm
Rogers Fund, 1912
The Metropolitan Museum of Art

In post-Islamic Persia, the Safavid dynasty ruled from 1501 until 1722 C.E. and established Shī'a imāms as their official religion. The gold ring on page 121 is from this era. It is unusual because of its massive bezel and shank. The raised round bezel is set with black jasper with a script engraving that reads, "He who guides towards the good is enough [reward] for the good." The underside is engraved with floral scrollwork filled with Kufic script that repeats the name of Ali four times.

The gilded silver and carnelian seal ring shown on the opposite page was worn by both sexes. Its carnelian stone was flat and had niello decoration on the inside of the setting. There are four corner prongs that resemble human figures. A similar ring, below it, was fashionable during the fifteenth century, when rings were worn on the little fingers. This signet ring is made of green nephrite, a less valuable kind of jade. On the seal is written "May you be free from all cares and anxieties in your possessions with (the help of) the most High! May the great wonders be

manifest! God aid you in calamities! May your life be without death!" The shanks of this ring have zoomorphic forms, and on the bezel it is beautifully written, "O my Lord! Instead of writing the name I say the following sentence. O my soul! In consequences of my love thy image is everywhere with me. O my soul! Be wise as wise in thy conversation as Solomon. My world and my heaven are in this ring." Inside the ring is written "Muhammad."

Coins were an important element in strings of beads, head ornaments, rings, and bracelets. Inscribed coins were acquired as mementos and were considered to be charms capable of offering protection against the Evil Eye. The use of coins as a decorative element in jewelry attests to the affinity between the two: like money, jewelry was legal tender and a symbol of social status.

Coin Used in a Pendant
Iraq, 9th to 11th century C.E.
Gold, gold dinar
D: 3 cm
Bequest of P. Balog, Rome
The Israel Museum, Jerusalem
IMJ 83.3.5476

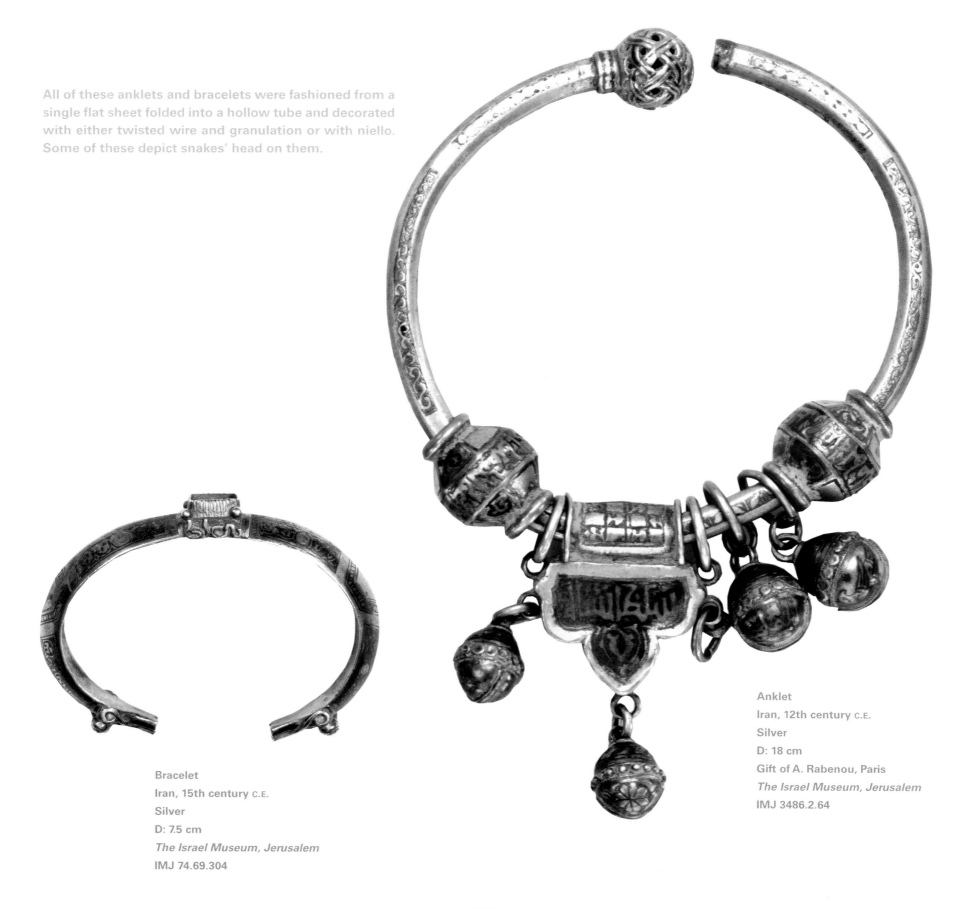

All of these anklets and bracelets were fashioned from a
single flat sheet folded into a hollow tube and decorated
with either twisted wire and granulation or with niello.
Some of these depict snakes' head on them.

Bracelet
Iran, 15th century C.E.
Silver
D: 7.5 cm
The Israel Museum, Jerusalem
IMJ 74.69.304

Anklet
Iran, 12th century C.E.
Silver
D: 18 cm
Gift of A. Rabenou, Paris
The Israel Museum, Jerusalem
IMJ 3486.2.64

124

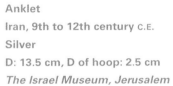

Anklet
Iran, 9th to 12th century C.E.
Silver
D: 13.5 cm, D of hoop: 2.5 cm
The Israel Museum, Jerusalem
IMJ 74.69.402

Bracelet
Iran, 12th to 13th century C.E.
Silver
D: 7.8 cm
The Israel Museum, Jerusalem
IMJ 74.69.305

Bracelet
Iran, 12th to 13th century
Silver
D: 8 cm
Gift of A. Rabenou, Paris
The Israel Museum, Jerusalem
IMJ 3498.2.64

This amulet is engraved with the words "God is the trust of Muhammad." There is a crescent moon above the inscription and a star of three short crossed strokes below it.

This amulet is engraved with two lines of cursive script that reads, "I have entrusted [my] cause to my maker."

Amulet Seal
Middle East, 10th to 12th century C.E.
Onyx
L: 15 mm, H: 11 mm, D: 4 mm
Private Collection

Amulet Seal
Middle East, 12th to 13th century C.E.
Green jasper
L: 15 mm, H: 11 mm, D: 3.5 mm
Private Collection

This amulet is engraved with the words, "And whosoever fears God" in cursive script.

Amulet Seal
Middle East, 18th to 19th century C.E.
Turquoise
L: 29 mm, H: 18.5 mm, D: 6 mm
Private Collection

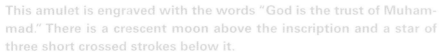

Amulets, which were first worn in Uruk during the fourth millennium B.C.E., continued to be used by Muslims. Calligraphy plays a big part of the design. On the opposite page is an amulet on which is written "God is the trust of Muhammad" with a crescent moon above the inscription and a star below. A turquoise oval cabochon also on the opposite page is inscribed with, "And whosoever fear God," which is from the Qur'an. On a straight-sided oval on the amulet pictured on the opposite page there are two lines of gilded calligraphy that says "I have entrusted (my) cause to my maker." Shown above is an extraordinary framed carnelian amulet with a pin on the back to make it usable as a brooch. The inscriptions are arranged inside a dome, on its flanking minarets, and around the border. While the amulets seen in this book are shown loose, they were often attached to a leather thong or worn on a gold chain for use in praying.

The cursive inscriptions of this amulet are broken up to make compartments, some arranged inside a dome and its flanking minarets, others around it and in the two parts of the central oval area and in the four compartments surrounding it.

Amulet Seal
Middle East, 19th century C.E.
Carnelian
L: 86 mm, H: 47 mm, D: 5 mm
Private Collection

DR. AUBREY BAADSGAARD

Aubrey Baadsgaard currently works in the Department of Anthropology at the University of Pennsylvania, where her focus is the Ancient Near and Middle East. She received both her B.A. and M.A. from Brigham Young University and her Ph.D. from the University of Pennsylvania. Dr. Baadsgaard has extensive field experience in Oman, the Abydos Survey Project in Abydos, Egypt; Wadi Mataha, Um Sihumm, Jordan; Khirbet al-Mudayna al-'Aliya, Smakeeya, Jordan; and Tell Dhiban, Dhiban, Jordan.

Why do people wear jewelry?

In our own society the topic of self adornment is of large appeal, as people of all walks of life strive to reflect prevailing social ideals of youthful beauty in their own appearances. Celebrities set the standards and are mimicked by others who wish to identify themselves with those considered the most beautiful and fashionable. Just as the fashion and style of contemporary cultural icons hold our interest, so too do the famous and royal personalities of the past, identified, in part, by their donning of the showy, glitzy, and expensive ornaments and jewels of the day. These important figures—heroes, kings, queens, and rulers—like present celebrities, created and showcased high fashion through the wearing of jewelry and ornaments.

Is there a type of jewelry central to your research?

It is these ancient fashion trendsetters who are the focus of my research on self adornment, specifically the jewelry worn by royal figures from ancient Mesopotamia (modern Iraq), the center of the world's oldest civilized society. Of particular interest to my study is the impressive set of jewelry found in the Ur Royal Cemetery and worn by sixteen important rulers buried with sacrificed court attendants.

Despite its great age, the jewelry collection from the Ur Royal Cemetery shows incredibly detailed workmanship. Gold pendants worn as part of head wreaths are made in the shape of leaves and chased with veins to give the appearance of living forms. Amulets are rendered in the detailed forms of bulls, fish, antelope, apple clusters, and date palms. Beads made of lapis lazuli, carnelian, gold, and silver were produced in standardized shapes and sizes and worn in abundance around the neck, body, and wrists. Gold and silver combs rose above the head of high-status women, and men wore headbands of gold chains and large gold beads. A queen named Pu-Abi wore 133 different ornament types, including 5,869 beads.

Who has made notable progress in the study of jeweled objects?

My attempt to re-envision personal adornment from the ancient past stands alongside many other efforts to resurrect notable identities by means of their jewelry and ornaments. For Lady Layard and Sophia Schliemann, both wives of famous nineteenth-century archaeological explorers—one the wife of Austin Henry Layard, excavator of the Assyrian capital of Nineveh, and the other the wife of Heinrich Schliemann, excavator of Troy—the recreation of ancient personalities occurred as they wore the ornaments of ancient royalty on themselves, thereby merging the splendorous identities of the past with their own. For Leonard Woolley, excavator of Ur, the renewal of past and glorious displays was best done through artistic recreations, such as through his wife's reconstructions of the head and face of one of the royal women from Ur, complete with hair, head ornaments, jewelry, and makeup. My own approach is to examine the sensorial and appreciable physical attributes of ornaments and jewelry, such as color, shape, size, location of wear, and manner of wear. By measuring and finding patterns in these properties, I have found that it is possible to reconstruct ancient fashion trends in ornament wearing and to trace the emergence, development, and change of such trends.

Since fashion is embedded within and linked with existing social and political institutions, reconstructing fashion trends provides great insight into the interworkings of ancient society and the creation of its peoples, materials, relationships, and experiences.

What is the social significance of jewelry?

My research on personal adornment demonstrates that the jewelry and ornaments, whether worn by those ancient or modern, are more than just

cultural accessories; they are central, even essential, parts of humanity. Jewelry and personal ornaments are ubiquitous across cultures distant in time and place, and yet they are so diverse in their forms, colors, and styles that they provide an intimate look into different ways of viewing, acting, and living in the world. Since jewelry is meant to be worn and to be seen, it provides for instant recognition of gender, status, and occupation, giving shape and color to ocial distinctions, roles, and relationships. Despite its potential for revealing much about society, jewelry and personal ornaments are currently under-used as sources of insight into some of humanity's most in-

teresting features. It is the intent of my research to highlight this potential by studying some of the richest collections of jewelry from the ancient world and thereby to demonstrate that ancient jewelry has much to reveal about the nature of human experience and what constitutes identity, culture, similarity and difference, and the means in which people engage in and understand the world.

Headdress of Queen Pu-Abi
Gold, lapis lazuli, and carnelian (displayed on
   a mannequin)
Ur, 2650–2550 B.C.E.
The University of Pennsylvania Museum
Image 152100

During this period certain styles for earrings emerged, including the basket-shaped and three-element earrings.

Single earring
Syria, 11th century C.E.
H: 3 cm, W: 1.5 cm
Lent by The Zucker Family, New York
The Israel Museum, Jerusalem
IMJ 85.53/1

Single earring
Iran, 12th century C.E.
Gold, quartz
H: 4.3 cm
Gift of Parviz Rabenou, New Jersey
The Israel Museum, Jerusalem
IMJ 1759.66

Single earring
Iran, 12th century C.E.
Gold, garnet
H: 4.3 cm
The Israel Museum, Jerusalem
IMJ 74.69.299

Islamic craftsmen placed a high value on colored stones such as rubies, emeralds, and pearls, and later in the fourteenth century C.E., turquoise and grey chalcedony. While the necklace on this page is not complete, the medallions are reminiscent of enameled Mughal pieces created to resemble most gems at only a fraction of the cost. It wasn't until the early 1800s that diamonds, emeralds, and rubies appear in Islamic jewelry, when nature, especially flowers and birds, remain prominent. The adaptation of precious stones, innovation of craftsmanship, and the evolution of creativity in subsequent centuries owes a debt to the millenia of ancient tradition.

Islamic jewelry brought in the use of colored stones.

Necklace elements
Iran, late 14th to early 15th century C.E.
Gold, turquoise, gray chalcedony, glass
Large medallion: H: 7.3 cm, W: 7 cm
Half medallion: H: 4.4 cm, W: 7 cm
Cartouches: H: 1.9 cm, W: 1.3 cm
Rogers Fund, 1989
The Metropolitan Museum of Art

BIBLIOGRAPHY

Ahlström, Gösta W. *The History of Ancient Palestine*. London: Sheffield Academic Press, 1994.

Ali, Wijdan. *The Arab Contribution to Islamic Art From the Seventh to the Fifteenth Centuries*. Cairo: The American University in Cairo Press, 1999.

Alizadeh, Saeed, et.al. *Iran: A Chronological History*. Tehran: Alhoda, 2003.

Amandry, P. *Collection Hélène Stathatos: Bijoux et Petits Objets*. Strasbourg: University of Strasbourg, 1971.

Aruz, Joan. *Art of the First Cities: The Third Millenium B.C. from the Mediterranean to the Indus (The Metropolitan Museum of Art Series)*. New Haven: Yale University Press, 2003.

Bachman, Hans-Gert. *The Lure of Gold: An Artistic and Cultural History*. New York: Abbeville Press, 2006.

Baldini Lippolis, Isabella. "L'Oreficeria Nell'Impero di Constantinopoli tra IV e VII Secolo." *Bibliotheca Archaeologica* 7 (1999): 96, 4.1, 1-8.

Basmachi, Faraj. *Treasures of the Iraq Museum*. Baghdad: Republic of Iraq, Ministry of Information, 1976.

Bendall, S. *Byzantine Weights: An Introduction*. London: Lennox Gallery, 1996.

Berkey, Jonathan P. *The Formation of Islam: Religion and Society in the Near East, 600-1800*. Cambridge: Cambridge University Press, 2003.

Bertman, Stephen. *Handbook to Life in Ancient Mesopotamia*. New York: Oxford University Press, 2003.

Binst, Olivier, et.al. *The Levant" History and Archaeology in the Eastern Mediterranean*. Cologne: Konemann, 1999.

Boehmer, R.M., F. Pedde and B. Salje. *Uruk: Die Gräber: Ausgrabungen in Uruk-Warka, Endberichte*. Mainz: Philipp von Zabern, 1995.

Brosius, Maria. *The Persians: An Introduction*. Oxon: Routledge, 2006.

Brown, Katherine Reynolds. *The Gold Breast Chain from the Early Byzantine Period in The Römisch-Germanisches Zentralmuseum*. Mainz: In Kommission bei R. Habelt, 1984.

Browning, Robert. *The Byzantine Empire*. Washington D. C.: The Catholic University of America Press, 1992.

Buckton, David. *Byzantium. Treasures of Byzantine Art and Culture from British Collections*. London: British Museum Press, 1994.

Burkert, Walter. *The Orientalizing Revolution: Near Easernt Influence on Greek Culture in the Early Archaic Age*. Cambridge: Harvard University Press, 1995.

Caubert, Annie and Marthe Bernus-Taylor. *The Louvre: Near Eastern Antiquities*. London: Scala Publications Ltd., 1991.

Collon, Dominique. *First Impressions: Cylinder Seals in the Ancient Near East*. London: British Museum Press, 2005.

Content, Derek J. *Islamic Rings and Gems: The Zucker Collection*. London: Phillip Wilson Publishers Ltd., 1987.

Christie, Agatha. *Murder in Mesopotamia*. New York: Dodd Mead and Company, 1936.

Culican, William. *The First Merchant Venturers: The Ancient Levant in History and Commerce*. London: Thames and Hudson, 1966.

Curatola, Giovanni, et. al. *The Art and Architecture of Mesopotamia*. New York: Abbeville Press, 2007.

Curtis, John E. and Nigel Tallis. *Forgotten Empire: The World of Ancient Persia*. London: The British Museum Press, 2005.

Curtis, John. *Mesopotamia and Iran in the Parthian and Sassanian Periods*. London: British Museum Press, 2000.

Dalton, O.M. "A Late Sassanian Silver Dish." *The Burlington Magazine for Connoisseurs* February 1922: 67, 69-70.

    Das Vorderasiatische Museum. Berlin: Staatliche Museen zu Berlin, 1992.

Davidson, P.F. and A. Oliver. *Ancient Greek and Roman Gold Jewelry in the Brooklyn Museum.* Brooklyn: The Brooklyn Museum, 1984.

Dennison, Walter. *A Gold Treasure from the Late Roman Period.* New York: Macmillan Co., 1918.

Deppert-Lippitz, Barbara. "L'opus Interrasile des Orfevres Romains in: Outils et Atelierd d'orfevres des Temps Anciens." *Antiquités Nationales, Mémoire 2* 1993: 69-72.

Dodd, Erica Cruikshank. *Byzantine Silver Stamps, in Dumbarton Oaks Studies VIII.* Washington, D.C.: Dumbarton Oaks, 1961.

————. *Byzantine Silver Treasure.* Berne: Abegg Stiftung Bern, 1973.

Ensoli, Serena and Eugenio La Rocca. *Aurea Roma. Dalla Città Pagana alla Città Cristiana.* Rome: L'Erma de Bretschneider, 2000.

Ettinghausen, Richard, Oleg Grabar and Marilyn Jenkins-Madina. *Islamic Art and Architecture 650-1250.* New Haven: Yale University Press, 2001.

Frye, Richard N. *The Golden Age of Persia.* London: Phoenix Press, 2000.

————. *The Heritage of Persia.* Cleveland: World Publishing Company, 1963.

Ghirshman, Roman. *Parthes et Sassanides.* Paris: Gallimard, 1962.

————. *Persian Art.* New York: Golden Press, 1962.

Gunter, Ann and Paul Jett. *Ancient Iranian Metalwork in the A. Sackler Gallery and the Freer Gallery of Art.* Washington, D.C.: Sackler Art Gallery, 1992.

Haller, Arndt. *Die Gräber und Grüfte von Assur.* Berlin: Gebr Mann, 1954.

Harper, Prudence Oliver. *The Royal Hunter: Art of the Sassanian Empire.* New York: The Asia Society, Inc., 1978.

Hasson, Rachel. *Early Islamic Jewellery.* Jerusalem: L.A. Mayer Memorial Institute for Islamic Art, 1987.

Hattstein, Markus and Peter Delius. *Islam Art and Architecture.* Cologne: Konemann, 2004.

Heinrich, Ernst. *Kleinfunde aus den archaischen Templeschichten in Uruk.* Berlin: Otto Harassowitz, 1936.

Hermitage Amsterdam. *Persia: Thirty Centuries of Art & Culture.* Hampshire: Ashgate Publishing, Limited, 2007.

Holy Bible: Authorized King James Version. Grand Rapids: The Zondervan Corporation, 1994.

Hunt, Norman Bancroft. *Historical Atlas of Ancient Mesopotamia.* New York: Checkmark Books, 2004.

Jenkins, Marilyn and Manuel Keene. *Islamic Jewelry in the Metropolitan Museum of Art.* New York: Metropolitan Museum of Art, 1983.

Kent, J.P.C. and K.S. Painter. *Wealth of the Roman World: AD 300-700.* London: British Museum Publications, 1977.

King, Philip J. and Lawrence E. Stager. *Life in Biblical Israel.* Louisville: Westminster John Knox Press, 2001.

Kitzinger, Ernst. *Byzantine Art in the Making.* Cambridge: Harvard University Press, 1995.

Kuhrt, Amélie. *The Ancient Near East, Volume I: From c. 3000 B.C to c. 1200 B.C.* London: Routledge, 1995.

Lexicon Iconographicum Mythologiae Classicae, Vol. VIII. Zurich: Artemis, 1997.

Limper, Klaudia. *Uruk: Perlen, Ketten, Anhänger, Grabungen 1912-1985.* Mainz: Philipp von Zabern, 1988.

Mango, Cyril. *The Oxford History of Byzantium.* Oxford: Oxford University Press, 2002.

Maxwell-Hyslop, K.R. *Western Asiatic Jewellery c 3000-612 BC.* London: Methuen & Co. Ltd, 1971.

Mazar, Amihai. *Archaeology of the Land of the Bible: 10,000-586 B.C.E.* New York: Doubleday, 1992.

Miller, J. Maxwell and John H. Hayes. *A History of Ancient Israel and Judah.* Louisville: Westminster John Knox Press, 2006.

Mitchell, T.C. *The Bible in the British Museum: Interpreting the Evidence.* London: The British Museum Press, 2004.

Moscati, Sabatino. *The Phoenicians.* New York: Rizzoli International Publications, Inc., 1999.

Musso, L. *Manifattura Suntuaria e Committenza Pagana nella Roma del IV Secolo: Indagine sulla Lanx di Parabiago.* Rome: L'Erma di Bretschneider, 1983.

Nemet-Nejat, Karen Rhea. *Daily Life in Ancient Mesopotamia.* Westport: Greenwood Press, 1988.

Niemeyer, B. "A Byzantine Gold Collar from Assiut: A Technological Study." *Jewellery Studies* Vol 8, 1998: 87-96.

Ogden and S. Schmidt. "Late Antique Jewelry: Pierced Work and Hollow Beaded Wire." *Jewellery Studies* Vol 4, 1990: 5-12.

Oldfather, C.H. *Diodorus of Sicily.* Cambridge: Harvard University Press, 2000.

Perrot, Georges and Charles Chipiez. *History of Art in Phoenicia and its Dependencies.* London: Chapman and Hall, Limited, 1885.

Pieridou, Angeliki. *Jewellery in the Cyprus Museum.* Cyprus: Nicosia: Republic of Cyprus, Ministry of Communications & Works, 1971.

Pirzio Biroli Stefanelli, Lucia. *L'Argento dei Romani. Vasellame da Tavoloa e D'Apparato.* Rome: L'Erma di Bretschneider, 1991.

Polk, Milbry and Angela M.H. Schuster. *The Looting of the Iraq Museum, Baghdad: The Lost Legacy of Ancient Mesopotamia.* New York: Harry N. Abrams, 2005.

Porada, Edith, et.al. *Art of Ancient Iran: Pre-Islamic Cultures.* New York: Crown Publishers, Inc., 1965.

Pritchard, James Bennett. *The Ancient Near East; An Anthology of Tests and Pictures.* Princeton: Princeton University Press, 1958.

Pritchard, James Bennett. *The Ancient Near East. Volume II: A New Anthology of Texts and Pictures.* Princeton: Princeton University Press, 1992.

Rawlinson, George. *Phoenicia: History of a Civilization.* London: I.B. Tauris & Co. Ltd., 2005.

Redford, Donald B. *Egypt, Canaan and Israel in Ancient Times.* Princeton: Princeton University Press, 1993.

Rosen-Ayalon, Myriam. *Islamic Art and Archaeology in Palestine.* Walnut Creek: Left Coast Press Inc., 2006.

Rosenthal, Renate. *Jewellery in Ancient Times.* London: Cassell & Company Ltd., 1973.

Ruxer, Mieczyslawa, et. al. "Bijouterie Antique de l'Ancienne Collection Czartoryski à Cracovie." *Archeologia Warszawa* 26 (1975): 113.

Science et Vie 972, September 1998: 47.

Tait, Hugh. *Seven Thousand Years of Jewellery.* London: British Museum Press, 2006.

Tallon, Francoise. *Les Pierres Precieuses de l'Orient Ancient: des Sumeriens aux Sassanides.* Paris: Editions de la Reunion des Musees Nationaux, 1995.

Weitzmann, Kurt and Margaret English Frazer. *Age of Spirituality: Late Antique and Early Christian Art Third to Seventh Century.* New York: The Metropolitan Museum of Art, 1977.

Wieshöfer, Josef. *Ancient Persia.* London: I.B. Tauris & Co. Ltd., 2001.

Zettler, Richard L., et. al. *Treasures from the Royal Tombs of Ur.* Philadelphia: Marquand Books, 1998.

PHOTOGRAPHY CREDITS

MUSEUM CREDITS

Page 67, Plaque with a King Holding a Sacred Tree, Princeton University Art Museum

Museum purchase, partial gift of Emily Townsend Vermeule, Honorary Degree Holder of the Class of 1989, and Cornelius Clarkson Vermeule III, in memory of

Francis F. Adams Comstock, Class of 1919 (1998-10)

Page 69, Pair of Openwork Bracteates in the form of Lions' Heads, Princeton University Art Museum

Museum purchase, Carl Otto von Kienbusch Memorial Collection Fund (2002-379/380)

Page 108, Roundel, The Metropolitan Museum of Art

The Alice and Nasli Heeramaneck Collection, Gift of Alice Heeramaneck, 1980

Page 118, Casket, The Metropolitan Museum of Art

Edward C. Moore Collection, Bequest of Edward C. Moore, 1891

Page 129, Headdress of Queen Pu-Abi, University of Pennsylvania Museum Objects B16692, B16693, B17709, B17710, B17711, B17711A, and B17712; image 152100

INDEX